W9-CEJ-577

1st EDITION

Perspectives on Modern World History

The Apollo 11 Moon Landing

1st EDITION

Perspectives on Modern World History

The Apollo 11 Moon Landing

Sylvia Engdahl

Editor

GREENHAVEN PRESS
A part of Gale, Cengage Learning

GALE
CENGAGE Learning

Detroit • New York • San Francisco • New Haven, Conn • Waterville, Maine • London

Christine Nasso, *Publisher*
Elizabeth Des Chenes, *Managing Editor*

© 2011 Greenhaven Press, a part of Gale, Cengage Learning.

Gale and Greenhaven Press are registered trademarks used herein under license.

For more information, contact:
Greenhaven Press
27500 Drake Rd.
Farmington Hills, MI 48331-3535
Or you can visit our Internet site at gale.cengage.com.

For product information and technology assistance, contact us at
Gale Customer Support, 1-800-877-4253.

For permission to use material from this text or product, submit all requests online at
www.cengage.com/permissions.

Further permissions questions can be e-mailed to permissionrequest@cengage.com.

Articles in Greenhaven Press anthologies are often edited for length to meet page requirements. In addition, original titles of these works are changed to clearly present the main thesis and to explicitly indicate the author's opinion. Every effort is made to ensure that Greenhaven Press accurately reflects the original intent of the authors. Every effort has been made to trace the owners of copyrighted material.

Cover image © Bettmann/Corbis and © Dennis Hallinan/Alamy .

LIBRARY OF CONGRESS CATALOGING-IN-PUBLICATION DATA

The Apollo 11 moon landing / Sylvia Engdahl, book editor.
    p. cm. -- (Perspectives on modern world history)
    Summary: "The Apollo 11 Moon Landing: Historical Background on the Apollo 11 Moon Landing; Controversies Surrounding the Apollo 11 Moon Landing; Personal Narratives"--Provided by publisher.
    Includes bibliographical references and index.
    ISBN 978-0-7377-5785-9 (hardback)
    1. Project Apollo (U.S.)--Juvenile literature. 2. Apollo 11 (Spacecraft)--Juvenile literature. 3. Space flight to the moon--Juvenile literature. I. Engdahl, Sylvia.
    TL789.8.U6A512112 2011
    629.45'4--dc22
                                                                    2011006222

Printed in the United States of America
1 2 3 4 5 6 7 15 14 13 12 11

CONTENTS

A. Bowdoin Van Riper

On July 20, 1969, men walked on the moon for the first time, fulfilling a centuries-old dream and ending the space race between the United States and the Soviet Union. Although this event represented a significant advance in technology, its major achievements were in science, as well as in restoring Americans' confidence and in bringing about a sense of unity among humankind.

Edward B. Lindaman

The first trip to the moon was not Apollo 11 but Apollo 8, which circled it on Christmas Eve 1968. Live television coverage was watched with enthusiasm and awe around the world, as for the first time in history Earth was seen as a whole and people of many nations expressed their feelings of unity.

on its immense significance to science and to the image of the United States around the world. It also explains that the landing demonstrated the need for manned rather than unmanned spacecraft, and proved that the human race has the capacity to seek a new environment if Earth ever becomes uninhabitable.

CHAPTER 2 Controversies Surrounding the Apollo 11 Moon Landing

A British historian explains how the view from the moon led people to focus on Earth rather than on space, to appreciate its beauty, and to become aware of the need to preserve it. This resulted in a reverence for the environment that has profoundly altered public attitudes toward the relationship between humans and nature.

was achieved by Americans no longer matters, he says. What will be remembered is that it showed that Earth must be seen globally.

CHAPTER 3   Personal Narratives

Russians reacted to it. Although it was not
kept secret from the public, it was not shown
on television and received little news coverage.

Robert L. Forward

An author of science fiction recalls how
thrilled he was by the Apollo moon landing,
how it made him feel part of the whole human
race, and how impressed he was at being able
to watch it live on television—something science fiction had never predicted.

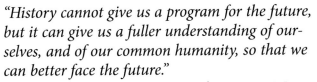

FOREWORD

"History cannot give us a program for the future, but it can give us a fuller understanding of ourselves, and of our common humanity, so that we can better face the future."

—Robert Penn Warren,
American poet and novelist

The history of each nation is punctuated by momentous events that represent turning points for that nation, with an impact felt far beyond its borders. These events—displaying the full range of human capabilities, from violence, greed, and ignorance to heroism, courage, and strength—are nearly always complicated and multifaceted. Any student of history faces the challenge of grasping the many strands that constitute such world-changing events as wars, social movements, and environmental disasters. But understanding these significant historic events can be enhanced by exposure to a variety of perspectives, whether of people involved intimately or of ones observing from a distance of miles or years. Understanding can also be increased by learning about the controversies surrounding such events and exploring hot-button issues from multiple angles. Finally, true understanding of important historic events involves knowledge of the events' human impact—of the ways such events affected people in their everyday lives—all over the world.

Perspectives on Modern World History examines global historic events from the twentieth-century onward by presenting analysis and observation from numerous vantage points. Each volume offers high school, early college level, and general interest readers a thematically arranged anthology of previously published materials that address a major historical event, with an emphasis on international coverage. Each volume opens with background information on the event, then presents the controversies surrounding that event, and concludes with first-person narratives from people who lived through the event or were affected by it. By providing primary sources from the time of the event, as well as relevant commentary surrounding the event, this series can be used to inform debate, help develop critical thinking skills, increase global awareness, and enhance an understanding of international perspectives on history.

Material in each volume is selected from a diverse range of sources, including journals, magazines, newspapers, nonfiction books, personal narratives, speeches, congressional testimony, government documents, pamphlets, organization newsletters, and position papers. Articles taken from these sources are carefully edited and introduced to provide context and background. Each volume of Perspectives on Modern World History includes an array of views on events of global significance. Much of the material comes from international sources and from US sources that provide extensive international coverage.

Each volume in the Perspectives on Modern World History series also includes:

- A full-color **world map**, offering context and geographic perspective.
- An annotated **table of contents** that provides a brief summary of each essay in the volume.
- An **introduction** specific to the volume topic.
- For each viewpoint, a brief **introduction** that has notes about the author and source of the viewpoint, and that provides a summary of its main points.
- Full-color **charts**, **graphs**, **maps**, and other visual representations.

- Informational **sidebars** that explore the lives of key individuals, give background on historical events, or explain scientific or technical concepts.
- A **glossary** that defines key terms, as needed.
- A **chronology** of important dates preceding, during, and immediately following the event.
- A **bibliography** of additional books, periodicals, and websites for further research.
- A comprehensive **subject index** that offers access to people, places, and events cited in the text.

Perspectives on Modern World History is designed for a broad spectrum of readers who want to learn more about not only history but also current events, political science, government, international relations, and sociology—students doing research for class assignments or debates, teachers and faculty seeking to supplement course materials, and others wanting to improve their understanding of history. Each volume of Perspectives on Modern World History is designed to illuminate a complicated event, to spark debate, and to show the human perspective behind the world's most significant happenings of recent decades.

INTRODUCTION

On July 20, 1969, humans set foot on another world for the first time. The landing of two American astronauts on the moon was watched on live television by 500 million people and was, at the time, widely described as a turning point in human history—an achievement that would be remembered in the distant future when all others of the twentieth century were forgotten. J.G. Crowther wrote that year in the magazine *New Scientist*, "The exploration of space is potentially of absolutely major importance. Its beginning marks the emergence of Man from the confines of the Earth, and can be compared with the original emergence of life from the primordial ocean; it sets a new stage for evolution."

Many people still believe as Crowther did. But for the majority of the public, the excitement of the moon landing has faded, and the Apollo moon program is often viewed as a mere side effect of the Cold War. To be sure, support for going to the moon was never as unanimous as the enthusiastic response to the television broadcast suggests. The day after the landing, the eminent playwright Arthur Miller wrote in the *New York Times*, "There are two schools of thought about the moon landing. One heralds it as the start of a new Age of Discovery like the period that began in 1492. The other regards it as a distraction from social problems. Few, though, feel anything but pride in the men who step over the astral frontier; even the crabbers are secretly envious of them." Hardly anyone foresaw that the moon would be so quickly abandoned. People expected that before the end of the century there would be a permanent base there, and probably a manned mission to Mars.

There were five more moon landings after Apollo 11, and three additional ones scheduled that were cancelled, despite their potential scientific value, because of the abrupt loss of public and congressional interest. The reasons for that loss are complex, and most are beyond the scope of this book. But among the major ones was the fact that the Space Race had been won. The goal had been to beat the Soviet Union to the moon, and once the nation had successfully reached it, many Americans saw no point in going there again.

Was the Apollo program simply a Cold War strategy? It was certainly funded on that basis; the money would not have been appropriated had not President John F. Kennedy persuaded Congress that it was important to the United States' image to be first in space. The Soviets had been ahead in the early years of spaceflight, with the first satellite, the first man in orbit, the first woman in space, the first multi-person crew, and the first space walk. They bragged that this showed communism was better than democracy and free enterprise, and other nations were impressed by their successes. It was deemed necessary for the United States to do more than catch up.

Historians disagree about how much effect the moon landing had on the outcome of the Cold War. Some think that despite the worldwide admiration of the achievement, it had little if any impact since the Russians were not as close to winning the race as NASA believed at the time. Others say that it was crucial because it proved to the Soviet Union that Americans could realize whatever advanced technology they set out to develop.

Throughout history, major technological developments that were funded and pursued during wartime—and which would not have been given priority otherwise—have turned out to be more significant to society later than they were in winning the war. The Cold War was no different from a shooting war in this respect. World War I produced aviation; World War II produced jet engines, radar, blood transfusion, and nuclear energy, to name a few; and the Cold War produced computer technology, as well as the space technology for the satellites on which communication now depends. All of these things are taken for granted today as essential to civilian life. The Apollo program itself demanded rapid advances in technology. The miniaturization of electronic components required for reaching the moon led to the invention of the integrated circuits (ICs) that make personal computers and cell phones possible.

The relative significance of the various benefits gained from going to the moon is controversial even among strong space advocates. A psychological advantage in the Cold War was one such benefit; technological advance was another; and the inspiration it offered to young people who later chose technical careers was still another. However, the moon program is most often assumed to have been justified by its value to science. NASA emphasized its scientific aims, which were not understood by the general public and in fact were not supported by the majority of scientists, who tended to feel that it diverted funds from their own fields of research. A 1964 poll of members of the American Association for the Advancement of Science found that 62 percent disagreed that "the vital national interests of the United States require that a high priority be given to landing a man on the moon by 1970." Since then, while some scientists say that only humans can deal with the unexpected factors any space mission is bound to involve, many have argued that unmanned space missions can achieve as much for science as manned ones. Nevertheless, the moon landings resulted in important scientific discoveries.

Only very few critics claim that the Apollo moon program did not have any beneficial results. The question, for most, is whether those results were worth the cost. The Apollo program cost about $25 billion in the 1960s, which would be well over $100 billion in today's dollars. Even taking into account the fact that this sum was spent not "in space" but on Earth, providing jobs for the nearly 5,000 people who worked on the project plus those who produced the materials it required, those were not the neediest people in the nation. Opponents of the moon landings maintain that it would have been better to devote the money to medical research or feeding the hungry.

Supporters of Apollo offer three main answers to that argument. In the first place, they say, the money would not have been spent on social programs, because Congress could not have been persuaded to allocate it for anything short of countering a perceived threat to the nation. Any funds saved by reducing the space budget would most likely have been devoted to other Cold War tactics.

Second, they point out that it is a fundamental characteristic of human beings to explore, to venture beyond the limits of their present environment, and that in the past this has always led to benefits far greater than could be foreseen. To deny this impulse would, in the opinion of many, be to suppress the essence of human nature. *Time* magazine, in an article published on December 6, 1968, suggested that both Americans and Russians "may well be driven toward the moon more by the age-old instincts of their species than by the most compelling of practical reasons."

This involves more than a desire for adventure. An editorial in the British magazine the *Economist* for July 19, 1969, expressed what many people still feel about the Apollo program:

> It should not be necessary, in a week such as this, to ask what it is all for. The pretext that men are sent into space for some form of intensive scientific investigation, yielding valuable information, has now been as good as dropped. The Russians are quite right: instruments do

that job as well, if not better than men, and certainly with less effort and anxiety. Instruments do not bleed. Men go into space for quite different reasons. They go especially to see whether it is the kind of place where other men, and their families and their children, can eventually follow them. A disturbingly high proportion of the intelligent young are discontented because they find the life before them intolerably confining. The moon offers a new frontier. It is as simple and splendid as that.

No one expects families and children to settle other worlds very soon, and many people wonder why anyone is even thinking about it when there are so many problems on Earth to be solved. Yet at the time of Apollo 11—and certainly since then—the strongest supporters of space exploration have viewed it as the first small but essential step toward reaching the stars. To them, the third and most compelling justification for that step was that travel to new worlds is a matter of the long-term survival of the human race. Aside from potential natural disasters that could destroy the Earth, many feel that there is danger of it becoming uninhabitable as a result of resource depletion, climate change, or a nuclear war. In the eyes of space settlement advocates, common sense dictates that a species should not remain confined to a single planet once it achieves the ability to establish outposts on others. In an essay on his website, astronaut John Young says, "NASA is not about the 'Adventure of Human Space Exploration,' we are in the deadly serious business of saving the species. All human exploration's bottom line is about preserving our species over the long haul."

In an unexpected way, concern for Earth's future was greatly magnified by the Apollo flights to the moon. The most profound result of those flights in terms of the effect on society was the emergence of the environmental movement. Previously, no one had ever been far enough from Earth to see it whole, as a sphere. When color pictures of it from a distance were obtained first by Apollo 8 and then by Apollo 11, people were stunned by how beautiful—and how small—it appears against the backdrop of space. The first reaction was simply that there are no dividing lines between nations and that surely, having looked at it in such a way, humankind should be able to live on it in peace. But before long, people also began to realize how unique and fragile its biosphere seems, and how necessary it is to preserve it. Had there been no flights beyond Earth orbit, this awareness might never have been acquired, and environmentalism might not have become the central issue that it is today.

Ironically, however, although the view of Earth from space united people in some ways, it has divided them in others. For some, it has strengthened the resolve not only to protect Earth's biosphere, but to reach out and enable humankind to become a spacefaring species before it is too late to ensure survival in case of disaster. Others have turned inward, away from space, declaring that Earth is the only part of the universe that humans ought to be concerned with. Thus there is now no consensus on whether there will or should be more trips to the moon and/or to Mars. Opinions on both sides are fueled by strong emotions, and in between is a large percentage of the public that simply does not care.

It is still too soon to say whether the Apollo moon landings will go down in history as the end of human space exploration or the beginning.

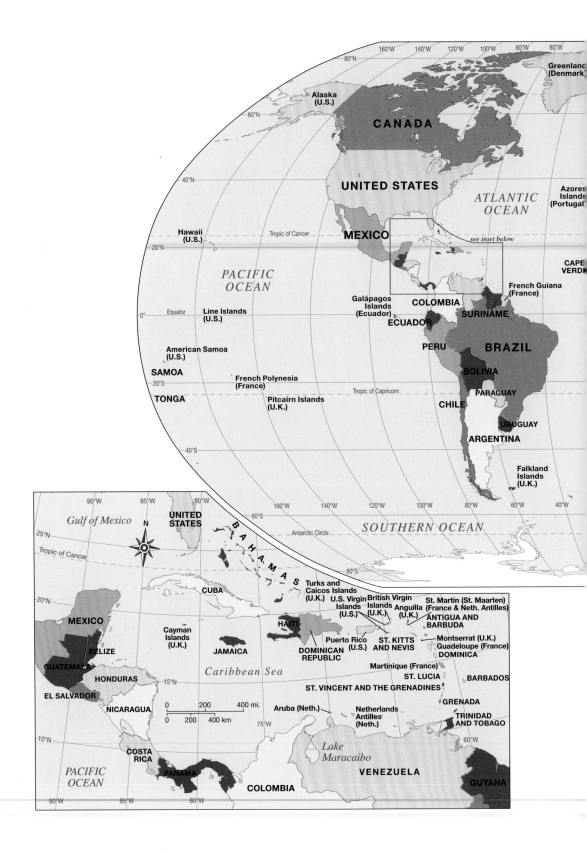

160°W 140°W 120°W 100°W 80°W 60°W

Greenland (Denmark)

80°N

Alaska (U.S.)

CANADA

60°N

UNITED STATES

ATLANTIC OCEAN

Azores Islands (Portugal)

40°N

Hawaii (U.S.)

Tropic of Cancer

MEXICO

see inset below

CAPE VERD

20°N

PACIFIC OCEAN

Galápagos Islands (Ecuador)

COLOMBIA

French Guiana (France)

SURINAME

Line Islands (U.S.)

Equator

0°

ECUADOR

PERU

BRAZIL

American Samoa (U.S.)

BOLIVIA

SAMOA

20°S

French Polynesia (France)

PARAGUAY

TONGA

Tropic of Capricorn

Pitcairn Islands (U.K.)

CHILE

URUGUAY

ARGENTINA

40°S

Falkland Islands (U.K.)

160°W 140°W 120°W 100°W 80°W 60°W 40°W

60°S

Antarctic Circle

SOUTHERN OCEAN

80°S

90°W 85°W 80°W

Gulf of Mexico N **UNITED STATES**

25°N

Tropic of Cancer

B A H A M A S

Turks and Caicos Islands (U.K.)

CUBA

U.S. Virgin Islands (U.S.)

British Virgin Islands (U.K.)

Anguilla (U.K.)

St. Martin (St. Maarten) (France & Neth. Antilles)

ANTIGUA AND BARBUDA

20°N

MEXICO

Cayman Islands (U.K.)

HAITI

Puerto Rico (U.S.)

ST. KITTS AND NEVIS

Montserrat (U.K.)

Guadeloupe (France)

DOMINICA

BELIZE

JAMAICA

DOMINICAN REPUBLIC

GUATEMALA

Caribbean Sea

Martinique (France)

ST. LUCIA

BARBADOS

HONDURAS

15°N

ST. VINCENT AND THE GRENADINES

EL SALVADOR

NICARAGUA

0 200 400 mi.

0 200 400 km

75°W

Aruba (Neth.)

Netherlands Antilles (Neth.)

GRENADA

TRINIDAD AND TOBAGO

10°N

Lake Maracaibo

60°W

COSTA RICA

PACIFIC OCEAN

PANAMA

VENEZUELA

GUYANA

COLOMBIA

90°W 85°W 80°W

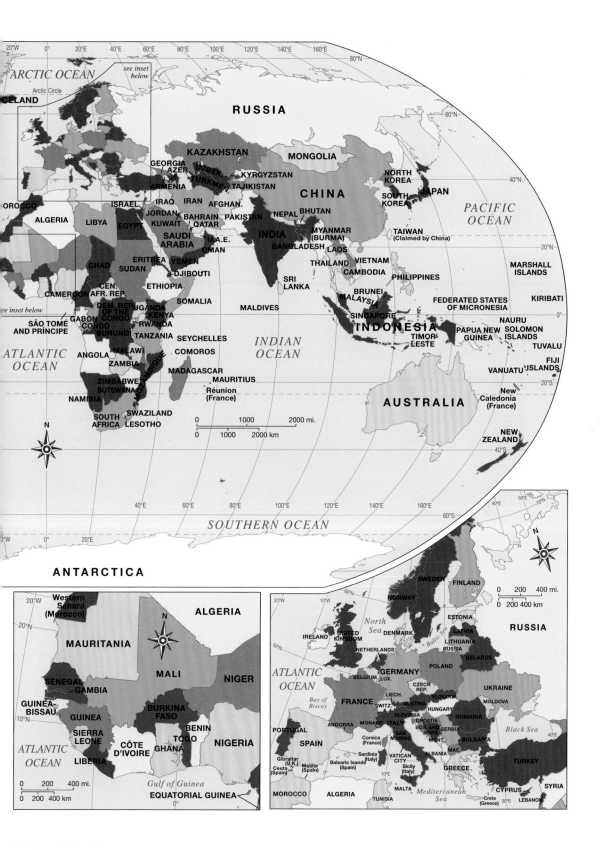

CHAPTER 1

Background on the Apollo 11 Moon Landing

An Overview of the Apollo 11 Moon Landing

A. Bowdoin Van Riper

Humans walked on the moon for the first time on July 20, 1969. Although this was a monumental achievement of technology, that was not its main significance. Rather, the moon landing ended the Soviet-American rivalry in space and symbolized a new hope of peace between nations, restored Americans' confidence after a decade of trouble, and led to significant scientific discoveries. Landing on a new world was seen as a triumph for all humankind. A. Bowdoin Van Riper is a historian of science and technology who teaches at Southern Polytechnic State University in Marietta, Georgia.

Photo on previous page: Millions in the United States and elsewhere followed Apollo 11's progress, from its July 16, 1969, launch onward. (Ralph Crane/Time & Life Pictures/Getty Images.)

On July 20, 1969, Neil Armstrong and Edwin "Buzz" Aldrin landed an ungainly spacecraft named *Eagle* on the moon and spent two hours

SOURCE. A. Bowdoin Van Riper, "The 1969 Moon Landing: First Humans to Walk on Another World," *Science and Its Times: Understanding the Social Significance of Scientific Discovery, Vol. 7.* Farmington Hills, MI: Gale, 2001. Copyright © 2001 by Gale. All rights reserved. Adapted and reproduced by permission.

exploring the lunar surface. They left the next day, rendezvousing in lunar orbit with the command ship *Columbia* and returning safely to Earth. The *Apollo 11* landing ended a decade of competition between the Soviet and American space programs, helped to restore the nation's self-confidence, and began an intensive program of exploration that transformed scientists' understanding of the moon.

Early Space Achievements

The dream of traveling to the moon was already centuries old when the Second World War ended in 1945. It had inspired Robert Goddard, who built and flew the first modern rockets in the New Mexico desert during the 1930s, and captivated Wernher von Braun, leader of a team that gave Nazi Germany the world's first guided missiles in 1944–45. Postwar Soviet and American leaders, recognizing the military potential of such missiles, clamored for bigger, more powerful versions. By 1957 the arms race had produced rockets strong enough to carry a nuclear bomb halfway around the world or a small satellite into Earth orbit. The Soviet Union launched such a satellite, *Sputnik I*, in October 1957. The success of *Sputnik* opened the Space Age and added a new dimension to the superpowers' already intense rivalry.

Soviet achievements in space overshadowed American ones from 1957 through April 1961, when Major Yuri Gagarin of the Red Air Force became the first human to orbit Earth. America's seemingly permanent second-place status in space stung the pride and undermined the Cold War foreign policies of the newly inaugurated president, John F. Kennedy. He proposed, in a May 1961 address to Congress, that the United States take a bold step: committing itself to landing a man on the moon and returning him safely to Earth by the end of the decade.

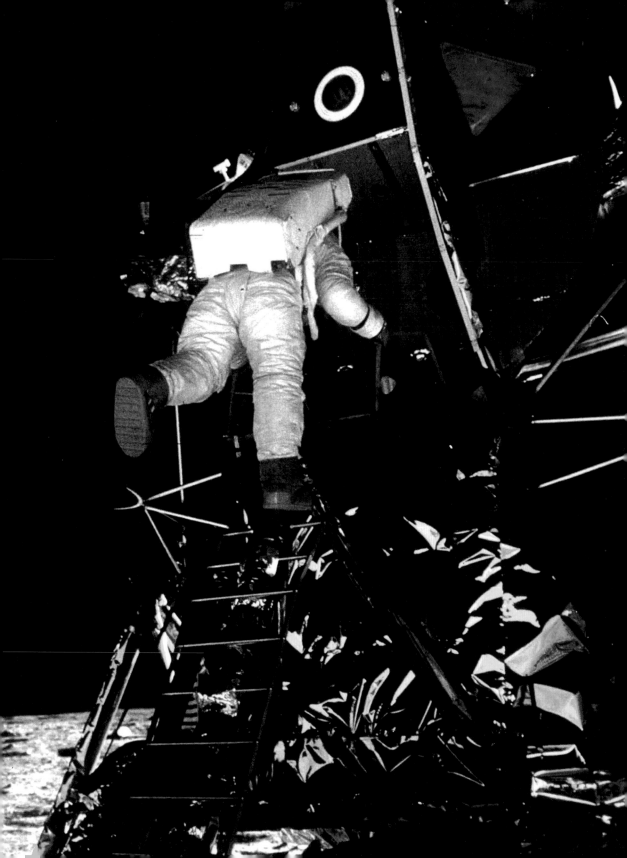

Project Apollo

The engineering and organizational challenges involved in meeting Kennedy's goal were immense. Project Apollo (as the moon-landing program came to be known) would involve flights a half-million miles long, taking as much as two weeks to complete. It would require boosters more powerful, guidance systems more accurate, and spacecraft more complex than any then in existence. It would also require the command ship and the lander to rendezvous and dock twice: once in Earth orbit, and once in lunar orbit. No such maneuver had even been planned, much less carried out, in 1961.

Designing, building, and testing the *Apollo* spacecraft and its massive Saturn V booster took six years, millions of government dollars and the combined efforts of America's leading aerospace manufacturers. Simultaneously, the National Aeronautics and Space Administration (NASA) conducted preparatory flights designed to lay the groundwork for *Apollo*. The ten flights of Project Gemini (1946–66) tested rendezvous techniques and crew endurance in Earth orbit. Three series of robot probes—Ranger, Surveyor and Orbiter—returned detailed information about the lunar surface, allowing NASA planners to select possible landing sites.

In January 1967, only weeks before the first manned test flight, Project Apollo suffered a tragic setback. Faulty wiring ignited a flash fire in the spacecraft during a routine launch simulation, killing astronauts Gus Grissom, Ed White and Roger Chafee. Extensively redesigned after the fire, the *Apollo* spacecraft would not fly with a human crew until late 1968. Once operational, however, it performed flawlessly. Two test flights in Earth orbit (*Apollo 7 and 9*) and two round trips to the moon (*Apollo 8 and 10*) proved its reliability, and gave NASA confidence to designate *Apollo 11* as the first lunar landing mission.

The July 20, 1969, lunar landing confirmed NASA's confidence in the *Apollo* spacecraft. Neil Armstrong's

Photo on previous page. Edwin "Buzz" Aldrin (pictured) and Neil Armstrong's walks on the Moon fulfilled individual, national, and human aspirations. (Apic/Getty Images.)

words as he jumped onto the surface of the moon were heard by millions of Americans and have since become the stuff of legend: "That's one small step for a man, one giant leap for mankind."

> The most significant results of Apollo 11 . . . were intangible rather than tangible—scientific and social rather than technological.

Impact of the Apollo Program

Many of the technologies developed for Project Apollo eventually found their way onto the consumer market: nonstick coatings, dehydrated foods, and miniaturized electronic components. NASA publicity often focused on such products in an effort to suggest that the space program provided taxpayers with tangible returns on their investment. These consumer spin-offs are, however, only the smallest part of Project Apollo's impact. The most significant results of *Apollo 11*, in particular, were intangible rather than tangible—scientific and social rather than technological.

The successful landing and return of *Apollo 11* ended the Soviet-American space race that had begun with *Sputnik* in 1957. No subsequent lunar landing could be as impressive as the first, Soviet planners recognized, and no other space achievement then within reach could have the same luster. A successful attempt to land a Soviet crew on the moon would bring only modest benefits; a failed attempt, on the heels of America's success, would be disastrous. The longstanding political and military rivalry between the superpowers was also diminishing at that time, making a continuation of the space race even more unlikely. New leaders and new diplomatic initiatives such as arms-control treaties created a temporary thaw in the Cold War. With competition giving way to a new spirit of superpower coexistence (known as détente), the space race seemed to belong to another era.

> After stepping onto the moon for the first time, Neil Armstrong's words were those of a human, not an American.

The words and symbols connected with the *Apollo 11* landing dramatized this shift in attitudes. They reflected little of the intense superpower rivalry that gave birth to Project Apollo in 1961. Instead, they embodied the new ideal of superpower coexistence. Armstrong and Aldrin had ample cause to gloat and to celebrate as they set foot on the moon, but they did neither. They planted their nation's flag where they landed but did not claim the land beneath it for their nation or their leaders. After stepping onto the moon for the first time, Neil Armstrong's words were those of a human, not an American. A metal plaque left behind to commemorate the landing expressed the idea even more clearly. "Here men from the planet Earth first set foot upon the moon . . . We came in peace, for all mankind."

Although the official symbols of *Apollo 11* did not define it as a specifically American triumph, most Americans saw it in just those terms. The year before the landing, 1968, had been one of the most turbulent in the nation's history. American forces suffered major setbacks in Vietnam; incumbent president Lyndon Johnson ended his bid for reelection; civil rights leader Martin Luther King was assassinated in April, and presidential hopeful Senator Robert Kennedy in June; protests against the Vietnam War grew increasingly angry and divisive; demonstrators and police fought in the streets of Chicago during the Democratic national convention. The series of successful *Apollo* missions that culminated in the landing of *Apollo 11* was welcome good news amid this string of national catastrophes. It was also proof, for those whose faith had begun to waver, that big government (NASA) and the American military (most of the astronauts) could still rise to greatness as they had during World War II.

President Kennedy's Historic Speech to Congress

I believe that this nation should commit itself to achieving the goal, before this decade is out, of landing a man on the moon and returning him safely to the earth. No single space project in this period will be more impressive to mankind, or more important for the long-range exploration of space; and none will be so difficult or expensive to accomplish. We propose to accelerate the development of the appropriate lunar space craft. We propose to develop alternate liquid and solid fuel boosters, much larger than any now being developed, until certain which is superior. We propose additional funds for other engine development and for unmanned explorations—explorations which are particularly important for one purpose which this nation will never overlook: the survival of the man who first makes this daring flight. But in a very real sense, it will not be one man going to the moon—if we make this judgment affirmatively, it will be an entire nation. For all of us must work to put him there.

SOURCE. *John F. Kennedy, Special Message to the Congress on Urgent National Needs, delivered in person before a joint session of Congress, May 25, 1961. www .jfklibrary.org.*

Apollo 11, in particular, also boosted Americans' confidence in their ability to solve society's problems. The moon landing became proof of American competence and achievement. "If we can send a man to the moon," a popular expression asked, "why can't we cure cancer, clean up the air, end poverty, etc.?"

NASA promoted the *Apollo 11* landing as the climax of a decade of hard work and as the fulfillment of the late President Kennedy's 1961 challenge. News commentators called it epoch-making and compared it to the European discovery of the New World. These attitudes encouraged Americans to see the first moon landing as a triumph for the human race in general and America in particular. The same attitudes, however, made the flight of *Apollo 11* a nearly impossible act for NASA to follow. Public interest in Project Apollo diminished sharply after the first landing, as did Congressional support. Three projected lunar landing missions—*Apollo 18*, *19*, and *20*—were cancelled for lack of such support. NASA undertook a variety of ambitious, successful missions in the three decades after *Apollo 11*, but few even came close to generating the same public interest or nationwide high spirits. NASA's desire to recapture the public confidence and substantial budgets it enjoyed in 1969 has, some critics charge, distorted its mission. Too often, they argue, the space agency neglects scientific research in order to fly missions that will draw public interest.

Scientific Discoveries

These criticisms, while valid to some extent, are also ironic. The *Apollo 11* landing itself made possible some of the most important science ever done in outer space. Neil Armstrong and Buzz Aldrin spent only a few hours on the lunar surface, deployed only a few scientific experiments, and collected only modest samples of lunar rock and soil. Because they were the *first* humans to walk on the moon, however, even these limited contributions vastly expanded scientists' understanding of it. The robot orbiters and landers that preceded *Apollo 11* provided close-up pictures of the lunar surface, but they could not assess its texture or chemical makeup. Pictures allowed Earth-bound geologists to form hypotheses about the moon but not to test them. Tests, and a clearer understanding of the moon's structure, composition, and age, required samples. The *Apollo 11* landing provided those samples and began a revolution in the earth sciences.

> A generation after Neil Armstrong took his 'one small step,' the legacy of *Apollo 11* remains very much alive.

Equally important, *Apollo 11* demonstrated that humans could make a soft landing on the moon, do useful work, and return safely to Earth. Premission concerns about possible hazards evaporated as the mission went on. Neither lander nor astronauts sank, as some had feared they would, into a thick layer of dust. Lunar soil did not burst into flames upon contact with oxygen. No alien microbes infected the returning astronauts. *Apollo 11* showed that the exploration of the moon was well within NASA's capabilities. Its success opened the door for later Apollo missions to concentrate on science, and as long as its budget allowed, NASA took full advantage of the opportunity. A generation after Neil Armstrong took his "one small step," the legacy of *Apollo 11* remains very much alive. Scientists' understanding of the moon is built almost entirely on data collected by the crews of *Apollo 11* and the five landing missions that followed. The landing remains a symbol of American greatness, and images of it were fixtures of century's-end retrospectives. And—for better or worse—NASA is still best remembered as the agency that put a man on the moon.

World Reaction to the Apollo 8 Flight Sets the Stage for Apollo 11

Edward B. Lindaman

Humans first traveled to the moon during the week of Christmas 1968, when the Apollo 8 astronauts circled it but did not land. It was during this mission that the globe of the Earth was seen by people for the first time in history, fostering a sense of the brotherhood of all humankind. People throughout the world were thrilled as they listened to the Christmas Eve message from lunar orbit, believing the event to be the beginning of a new era of peaceful exploration. This viewpoint was written prior to the Apollo 11 moon landing. During the time of the Apollo missions, Edward B. Lindaman was director of program control for North American Rockwell's space division. Later, he was president of Whitworth College in Spokane, Washington.

SOURCE. Edward B. Lindaman, *Space: A New Direction for Mankind*, pp. 131–34, 146–47. Copyright © 1969 by Edward B. Lindaman; renewed © 1997 by Edward B. Lindaman. Reprinted by permission of HarperCollins Publishers.

The Kremlin phoned the White House, asking to be kept informed via the Washington-Moscow hot line; and the President's staff did so. Meanwhile history's biggest television audience stared at pictures broadcast live to networks across Europe, Japan, and North and Central and South America. What was happening? What conceivable event could catch interest around the world, among statesmen and housewives and peons alike?

The event, of course, was the epochal voyage of Apollo 8 in Christmas week of 1968: a long-awaited journey unlike any before it in Earth's long history. For seven years *genus homo* [human beings] had edged into the eternal cold of Space, soaring as high as 853 miles above the ground. Now at last he was making the great escape from his own planet. Reporters from forty nations gathered at Cape Kennedy to watch the mighty rocket rise.

The astronauts [Frank] Borman, [William] Anders, and [James] Lovell were fulfilling mankind's oldest dream and universal myth. The urge to soar free, to explore the unknown, to visit an another celestial body, is as old as the legends of Icarus and Diana.[1] People of all kinds have this in common, and so on December 21, 1968 their hearts soared into Space, following the rocket on its long, wild way to the moon.

As President [Lyndon] Johnson remarked afterward, "For seven days the Earth and all who inhabit it knew a measure of unity through these brave men. . . . These men represented in the vastness of Space all mankind, all its races, all its nationalities, all its religions, all its ideologies."

The First Sight of Earth

On their translunar passage the astronauts aimed a television camera and sent back stunning pictures of a great heavenly body no man had ever seen before—because none had ever left it. And as the state of Texas, Florida,

California, or Alaska vanished into cloud seas—as the United States shrank to a misted island, as Africa and Europe and Asia merged and the entire planet Earth became a single lovely sphere—the sight set many people to thinking one thought.

The thought was best expressed, perhaps, by the poet Archibald MacLeish: "To see the Earth as it truly is . . . is to see ourselves as riders on the Earth together, brothers on that bright loveliness in the eternal cold—brothers who know now they are truly brothers." Others said the same in different words. A German lecturer in war studies at the University of London wrote: "The remarkable pictures of the Earth taken from near the moon's surface impress on us the utter ridiculousness of the nature and substance of man's quarrels with man . . . and the tendency, particularly among younger people, to see the world's problems as a whole, regardless of national or regional confines." Norman Cousins, widely known editor and worker for peace, wrote: "It is possible that the most effective and imaginative thing the United States could do at Paris (in the Vietnam war negotiations) would be to send over the astronauts of Apollo 8 as our negotiators. The astronauts have seen the Earth whole, something the statesmen have yet to do."

The Christmas Eve Telecast

As the dreaming moon raced below them on Christmas Eve, the astronauts talked and the world heard. Space, hundreds of thousands of miles of Space, and these voices pulsing through it, finding their way back to Earth and quickening men's hearts.

What could the astronauts say at this milestone in history, as the human family felt itself moving toward a strange new destiny? What would be worth hearing by the peo-

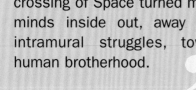

It was remarkable how this crossing of Space turned men's minds inside out, away from intramural struggles, toward human brotherhood.

ples of the globe with their parliaments, their temples, their armies, their corporations, their farms? Bill Anders wrote later:

> We thought a long time about that, and I personally changed my mind. I first thought we should use something Christian, something about Christmas. But when we thought about the vastness of our world, we decided to read a message that did not belong to any one religion but which belonged to all men on Earth, the story of our creation.

And so the astronauts spoke perhaps the most fitting words imaginable, the majestic opening passage of the Book of Genesis: "In the beginning God created . . . "

And Frank Borman signed off with a prayer: "O God . . . show us what each of us can do to set forth the coming of the day of universal peace."

These religious thoughts, at the height of a great scientific mission, proved to be widely shared. It was remarkable how this crossing of Space turned men's minds inside out, away from intramural struggles, toward human brotherhood and toward a God whose unimaginable complexity had generated galaxies and atoms and thinking humans. The Astronauts' humble words were rebroadcast in many languages over radio networks in the free world and Communist world alike. Even Red Hungary, one of the most totalitarian of governments, interrupted its radio and television programs for Apollo broadcasts.

Joy Around the World

As the little ship completed its ten orbits of the moon and turned homeward, a top Soviet Space scientist told newsmen, "This goes beyond a national achievement. It marks a stage in the development of the universal culture of Earthmen." And when the ship came down from the silent gulfs of Space and landed safe on Earth again, a wave of joy ran around the globe. Warm messages poured in by the thousands to the Manned Spacecraft Center in Texas. Ten Soviet cosmonauts wired congratulations, concluding: "We wish you further success on all other flights. We are confident future exploration of Space will greatly benefit Earthly men."

An American foreign correspondent reported from Paris: "Moon flight has changed the atmosphere. Americans on the streets, in the shops, everywhere, get French congratulations." A reporter in London wrote, "The American public performance invites the whole world to take part."

The invitation was reiterated and stressed in Washington. As he presented medals to the returned spacefarers, President Johnson said:

We have learned how men and nations may make common cause in the most magnificent and hopeful enterprises.

We in the United States are already engaged in cooperative space activities with more than 70 nations. We have proposed a variety of adventures to expand international partnership in Space exploration. . . .

If there is an ultimate truth to be learned from this historic flight, it may be this: There are few social or scientific or political problems which cannot be solved by men, if they truly want to solve them together. . . .

International Cooperation

Reaching out from Washington to the ends of the Earth, NASA is zealous and many-sided in its assigned mission of "cooperation with other nations for the benefit of all mankind." It is working with 80 governments from Ascension Island to Zambia in various Space experiments. It exchanges scientific papers with 240 institutions in 41 countries. Each year it launches about 150 sounding rockets in collaborative probes, with other countries, of the layers of airspace above their own lands. It has helped Canada, Japan, France, Germany, and Great Britain design and launch at least 24 satellites.

More than 400 Space scientists and technicians from 14 countries have flocked to America for training in NASA facilities, at their own or their government's expense. NASA's vast variety of off-the-shelf electronic equipment is often rented to foreign experimenters, freeing them from laborious tasks of building their own; and NASA's computers give them quick analyses of experimental results.

In part because of the magnetism of our Space programs, 130,000 foreign students are now in US schools and universities, compared with only 35,000 in 1954. Of these, 1,300 earned Ph.D.'s in Space-related studies in 1968. NASA encouraged their progress by helping universities build research facilities, and sometimes by providing scholarships or research grants.

The astronauts of Apollo 8 blazed the trail for the 1969 lunar landing by orbiting the moon in 1968. (AP Images.)

NASA's beneficences are not one-way. Fifteen countries maintain tracking stations that NASA needs for noting its satellites' courses and performance. Italy's unique San Marco launch platform, peculiarly valuable because it is near the equator, is available to NASA. The European Space Research Organization and 21 nations now trade data with NASA.

Test samples from the moon's surface, borne home by Apollo crews, are to be shared with 135 scientists from 8 foreign countries. In this sense the moon exploration program is truly international. But NASA hopes

> Beyond their hopes of gain, governments and common people are drawn together by the sheer romantic fascination of thinking about Earthmen on the lunar surface.

to be more polyglot still. It wants to enroll men of other countries in the most exclusive and most glamorous apprenticeship the world has ever known: the apprenticeship of NASA astronauts.

The Dawn of a New Era

When nations do constructive jobs together they brighten the prospects of peace. Their joint activities in Space are among the most hopeful enterprises in history, for they foster world prosperity. A prosperous world tends to be a peaceful world. But beyond their hopes of gain, governments and common people are drawn together by the sheer romantic fascination of thinking about Earthmen on the lunar surface, and of looking ahead up the path to the planets. They feel themselves pulled along by an irresistible historical process, the fulfillment of one era, the dawn of another—an intuitive public certainty that the world has outgrown one way of life and is starting afresh, just as it did when the opening of the New World broke the long imprisonment of the Middle Ages.

Note

1. In Greek mythology, Icarus attempted to escape Crete by flying with wings made by his father. Ignoring instructions not to fly too close to the sun, Icarus fell to his death. Diana is associated with the moon in Roman mythology.

Millions Throughout the World Tuned in to the Moon Landing Broadcast

Associated Press

People all over the world watched the moon landing on television—or, if they had no access to television, listened on the radio. Only in Communist countries was it not broadcast. World leaders sent their congratulations, commenting on the event's significance to history and the hope that it would unite humankind in peace. The vast majority of people were awed and elated by it, although there was unfavorable response in a few places such as Cuba. The following is an Associated Press news story that appeared in papers nationwide.

SOURCE. "Millions Around Globe Hung on Every Word from Astros," *Herald-Star* (Stebenville, Ohio), July 21, 1969. Copyright © 1969 by The Associated Press. All rights reserved. Reproduced by permission.

Laplanders [Scandinavian aboriginal people] pasturing their reindeer listened on transistor radios. Japanese stayed up all night to watch on television. Millions around the world hung on every word from the two U.S. astronauts walking on the moon.

In some countries many remained unaware. Communist China, with one quarter of the world's population, did not broadcast news about Apollo 11, nor did North Vietnam or North Korea.

As Neil A. Armstrong's boots scuffed the lunar dust, it was just before sunrise in most of Europe and a crowd of 2,000 still clustered around a giant television screen in London's Trafalgar Square.

At the Jodrell Bank radio observatory, Sir Bernard Lovell, Britain's leading space expert, stopped tracking the progress of the Soviet craft Luna 15 over the moon to watch Armstrong.

"I'm just speechless with amazement," Lovell said. "There is nothing more I can say than that it is absolutely fantastic. One can scarcely believe it is taking place as one sees it."

> Crowds in front of TV screens at Paris sidewalk cafes and bars in Rome cheered as [Neil] Armstrong bounded over the moon's surface and Buzz Aldrin began his descent.

Crowds Cheer

Crowds in front of TV screens at Paris sidewalk cafes and bars in Rome cheered as Armstrong bounded over the moon's surface and Buzz Aldrin began his descent.

There was no word from the Vatican on whether Pope Paul VI stayed up to watch the walk, but when the astronauts landed the 71-year-old pontiff hailed them as "conquerors of the moon." He said man faces "the expanse of endless space and a new destiny."

In Venezuela, today is a national holiday, and the bells of hundreds of churches pealed during the walk. A

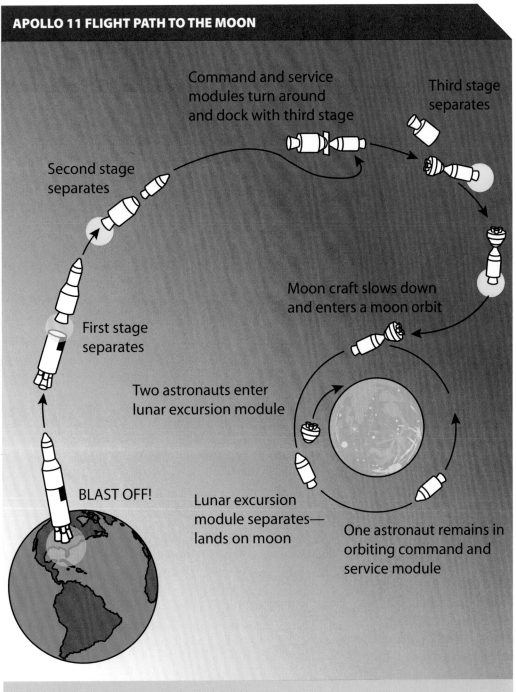

APOLLO 11 FLIGHT PATH TO THE MOON

Command and service
modules turn around
and dock with third stage

Third stage
separates

Second stage
separates

First stage
separates

Moon craft slows down
and enters a moon orbit

Two astronauts enter
lunar excursion module

BLAST OFF!

Lunar excursion
module separates—
lands on moon

One astronaut remains in
orbiting command and
service module

Taken from: "Making the Modern World," The Science Museum, 2004.

Japanese girl in Tokyo said as she watched a streetside monitor. "It's like a dream, although I know it's not a dream."

One Yugoslav teen-ager sounded a dissent: "They have stolen the romance out of the moon and it will never be the same again. Now the moon is real, and lovers won't have it for themselves alone anymore."

> At headquarters bases and other rear areas in Vietnam, Americans gathered around radios at midmorning to hear the broadcast of the walk.

Folk Poems Composed

In arctic Norway where the midnight sun kept skies bright through the night, Laplanders sat around their campfires composing sing-song folk poems about the astronauts as they listened to their transistors.

Poles jammed the lobby of the U.S. Embassy in Warsaw while hundreds applauded outside. Soviet media reported the landing without fanfare, but many Russians undoubtedly stayed up to listen to Western broadcasts about the exploration.

Pravda, the Soviet Union's leading newspaper, gave the U.S. moon triumph only a small headline above a small story near the bottom of the front page.

In a more prominent place at the top of the page was a larger story on the shift of Luna 15, the unmanned Soviet spacecraft, closer to the moon. *Pravda* still gave no hint what Luna 15's mission was.

At headquarters bases and other rear areas in Vietnam, Americans gathered around radios at midmorning to hear the broadcast of the walk, as did the staff at the U.S. Embassy in Saigon.

First Steps Broadcast

In the war-torn Middle East, Cairo Radio broadcast news about the first steps before reviewing Sunday's fierce air battle with Israel.

One night club owner in Beirut stopped a striptease act to tell the audience, "We've made it."

In Australia it was lunchtime when the astronauts stepped onto the moon. From the cities to the lonely cattle stations in the moon-like Outback, Australians regarded the lunar exploration with awe. Australian newspapers highlighted their "kangaroo" movements.

For many people in the Asian subcontinent and Africa, the Voice of America broadcast [a broadcasting service funded by the US government] was the only means of hearing about the two astronauts.

Thousands of Europeans without TV sets spent the night at friends' houses to follow the lunar adventure.

A crowd in Berlin, Germany, watches the Apollo 11 space mission through the window of a TV store. Television sets were not yet commonplace, and people watched news of the mission wherever they could. (**Edwin Reichert/ AP Images.**)

The Flag and Plaque on the Moon

In January of 1969, President Richard M. Nixon's inaugural address stressed the international flavor of the Apollo program. "As we explore the reaches of space, let us go to the new worlds together—not as new worlds to be conquered, but as a new adventure to be shared." NASA officials noted the tone of the speech, and there was some discussion within the agency that a United Nations flag could be used for the flight. This was one of the possibilities considered by the Committee on Symbolic Activities for the First Lunar Landing. . . . The committee was instructed to select symbolic activities that would not jeopardize crew safety or interfere with mission objectives; that would "signalize the first lunar landing as an historic forward step of all mankind that has been accomplished by the United States" and that would not give the impression that the United States was "taking possession of the moon" in violation of the Outer Space Treaty. . . .

The committee's report recommended using only the flag of the United States during the lunar extravehicular activity (EVA). In addition, the committee suggested that a plaque bearing an inscription ("Here men from the planet Earth first set foot upon the moon July 1969, A.D. We came in peace for all mankind") be mounted on the lunar module to emphasize that the purpose of the mission was one of exploration and not conquest. The original plaque design featured a U.S. flag, but the graphic was changed to pictures of the eastern and western hemispheres of the Earth to symbolize the crew's point of origin. It was decided that, in addition to the large flag, 4 x 6 inch flags of the 50 states, the District of Columbia, the U.S. territories, and flags for all member countries of the United Nations and several other nations, would be carried in the lunar module and returned for presentation to governors and heads of state after the flight. . . .

Because the final decision to fly the flag and attach the plaque was made so close to the launch date, a Lear jet was chartered to fly . . . the flag assembly and the commemorative plaque to KSC [Kennedy Space Center] before the launch. The flag and plaque were installed on the lunar module of Apollo 11 at 4:00 in the morning as the spacecraft sat atop its Saturn V rocket ready for launch.

SOURCE. *Anne M. Platoff, "Where No Flag Has Gone Before: Political and Technical Aspects of Placing a Flag on the Moon," NASA Contractor Report 188251, August 1993. www.jsc.nasa.gov/history/flag/flag .htm.*

In Fife, Scotland, a boy born Sunday night was to be named Neil Edwin Michael—the second child in Britain to be named after all three astronauts.

On British television Sunday night David Threlfall, who bet $24 five years ago that man would set foot on the moon before 1971, received a check for $24,000 even though Armstrong hadn't left the lunar module yet.

A spokesman for the London bookmaker William Hill, with whom Threlfall placed the bet at 1,000-1 odds when he was 26, said the touchdown was "good enough for us."

Admiration Expressed

As newspapers prepared special editions with huge headlines, world leaders went on television to express their admiration and sent congratulatory cables to President [Richard] Nixon.

Prime Minister Harold Wilson of Britain called it a "most historic scientific achievement in the history of man" and told his audience: "Above all we must pay tribute to the heroism and fortitude of the men who are out there and to the men who have gone before them."

President Guiseppe Saragat of Italy said: "Of all the sentiments that stir us, gratitude toward the American people dominates, that people formed by innumerable immigrants from every country, that has given humanity so great a victory."

Indian Prime Minister Indira Gandhi said: "The moment of triumph and achievement is also a moment of humility and self-search. . . . Let us direct this power of man which soars starward into strengthening the bonds of peace and brotherhood on earth."

Not all the reaction was favorable.

In Havana, where the Voice of America broadcast went unjammed, one Cuban industrial worker, Luis Sosacotilla, 43, said: "Their experiment does nothing to benefit humanity." He said the money should have been used to wipe out poverty and misery in the United States, a reflection of the government view on Apollo.

Klaus Bahnke, president of West Germany's Radical Socialist German Students Federation, said he and his colleagues were avoiding the news "because they are only trying to cover up the real goals of the United States."

A British Newspaper Describes What the Astronauts Did on the Moon

Times (London)

On July 20, 1969, the day of the Apollo 11 moon landing, the *Times* of London devoted its entire front page to the story, and in 2007 it reprinted the following excerpts from that coverage. They describe in detail what the astronauts did during the two hours they were on the moon and what was seen and heard by the watchers on Earth.

Neil Armstrong became the first man to take a walk on the moon's surface early today [July 20, 1969]. The spectacular moment came after he had inched his way down the ladder of the fragile lunar

> "There were tense moments in the mission control centre at Houston while they awaited news of the safe landing."

bug Eagle while colleague Edwin Aldrin watched his movements from inside the craft. The landing, in the Sea of Tranquillity, was near perfect and the two astronauts on board Eagle reported that it had not tilted too far to prevent a take-off. The first word from man on the moon came from Aldrin:

"Tranquillity base. The Eagle has landed."

Of the first view of the lunar surface, he said: "There are quite a few rocks and boulders in the near area which are going to have some interesting colours in them." Armstrong said both of them were in good shape and there was no need to worry about them. They had experienced no difficulty in manoeuvring the module in the moon's gravity. There were tense moments in the mission control centre at Houston while they awaited news of the safe landing. When it was confirmed, one ground controller was heard to say; "We got a bunch of guys on the ground about to turn blue. We're breathing again." Ten minutes after landing, Aldrin radioed: "We'll get to the details of what's around here. But it looks like a collection of every variety, shape, angularity, granularity; a collection of just about every kind of rock." He added: "The colour depends on what angle you're looking at . . . rocks and boulders look as though they're going to have some interesting colours."

It was 3.56 A.M. (British Standard Time) when Armstrong stepped off the ladder from Eagle and on to the moon's surface. The module's hatch had opened at 3.39 A.M.

"That's one small step for [a] man but one giant leap for mankind," he said as he stepped on the lunar surface. [The "a" was not heard because of static.]

The two astronauts opened the hatch of their lunar module at 3.39 A.M. in preparation for Neil Armstrong's walk. They were obviously being ultra careful over the operation for there was a considerable time lapse before Armstrong moved backwards out of the hatch to start his descent down the ladder. Aldrin had to direct Armstrong out of the hatch because he was walking backwards and could not see the ladder.

> When the television cameras switched on there was a spectacular shot of [Neil] Armstrong as he moved down the ladder.

Setting Foot on the Lunar Surface

Armstrong moved on to the porch outside Eagle and prepared to switch the television cameras which showed the world his dramatic descent as he began to inch his way down the ladder.

By this time the two astronauts had spent 25 minutes of their breathing time but their oxygen packs on their backs last four hours.

When the television cameras switched on there was a spectacular shot of Armstrong as he moved down the ladder. Viewers had a clear view as they saw him stepping foot by foot down the ladder, which has nine rungs. He reported that the lunar surface was a "very fine-grained powder."

Clutching the ladder Armstrong put his left foot on the lunar surface and reported it was like powdered charcoal and he could see his footprints on the surface. He said the L.E.M.'s [lunar module] engine had left a crater about a foot deep but they were "on a very level place here." Standing directly in the shadow of the lunar module Armstrong said he could see very clearly. The light was sufficiently bright for everything to be clearly visible.

The next step was for Aldrin to lower a hand camera down to Armstrong. This was the camera which Armstrong was to use to film Aldrin when he descended from Eagle. Armstrong then spent the next few minutes taking photographs of the area in which he was standing and then prepared to take the "contingency" sample of lunar soil. This was one of the first steps in case the astronauts had to make an emergency take-off before they could complete the whole of their activities on the moon.

Armstrong said: "It is very pretty out here." Using the scoop to pick up the sample, Armstrong said he had pushed six to eight inches into the surface. He then reported to the mission control centre that he placed the sample lunar soil in his pocket.

The first sample was in his pocket at 4.08 A.M. He said the moon "has soft beauty all its own" like some desert of the United States. Armstrong then started to prepare to guide Aldrin out of the lunar module as he emerged backwards through the hatch on the porch.

By this time Armstrong and Aldrin had used up 45 minutes of their oxygen supply. Armstrong told Aldrin: "I feel very comfortable and walking is very comfortable. You've got three steps to go and then the long one."

Seconds later Aldrin dropped down on to the lunar surface and Armstrong said: "Isn't that wonderful." It was 4:15 [A.M.] when Aldrin stepped on to the surface. One astronaut was heard saying "magnificent desolation."

Moving Around in Low Gravity

Armstrong and Aldrin then carried out a number of exercises. Armstrong could be seen jumping up and down while Aldrin, clutching the ladder, was doing what looked like a knees bend. Armstrong appeared to move rapidly across the moon's surface but only seeming to take short steps.

Sharp contrast between light and shadow made the television picture partly obscure, but early overall transmission was good. One of the astronauts reported that the rocks had a powdery surface and were rather slippery. One of them said that he intended to lose balance in one direction but recovery was quite natural. He said you had to lean in the direction you wanted to go.

One Small Step for (a) Man

There has been controversy surrounding the "a" in [Neil Armstrong's] statement. People on Earth heard him say, "That's one small step for man, one giant leap for mankind." Historians assumed that he bungled the words and Armstrong himself was unsure. He certainly knew what he meant to say. The missing "a" was recovered in 2006 through modern acoustical evidence. A computer analysis of Armstrong's transmission from the Moon was done by Peter Shann Ford, a Sydney, Australia-based computer programmer. It provides convincing proof that the "a" was hidden in some static during the transmission: "That's one small step for (a) man, one giant leap for mankind." James R. Hansen, Armstrong's authorized biographer, presented the findings to Neil Armstrong. Presentations were next made at the Smithsonian Institution's Air and Space Museum in Washington, D.C., and at NASA's Washington headquarters.

SOURCE. *Tahir Rahman, ed.,* We Came in Peace for all Mankind: The Untold Story of the Apollo 11 Silicon Disc. *Leathers Publishing, 2008, p. 42.*

The astronauts reported to mission control that their steps tended to sink down about [a] quarter of an inch. All the time the two astronauts could be seen moving around in front of the lunar module. Their movements were slow and they seemed to lope.

They then unveiled the plaque which contained President Nixon's signature and with an inscription saying: "Here men from the planet Earth first set foot upon the moon July, 1969, A.D. We came in peace for all mankind."

Apollo 11's successful landing on the moon filled newspaper front pages worldwide. (Popperfoto/Getty Images.)

The two astronauts then removed the television camera from the storage compartment in the lower half of the lunar module. As they carried the camera away from the module they pointed it towards the ground to show the first view of the lunar surface. One of the astronauts asked:

"Have I got plenty of cable?" The other replied: "You have got plenty."

After Armstrong had moved about 50 feet from the module, Aldrin said: "Why don't you turn round?" The camera then swung round and for the first time viewers saw a full view of the module as it nestled on the lunar surface. Aldrin said he was "filled with admiration" at their first-in-a-lifetime sight and experience.

Taking Pictures on the Moon

Armstrong turned the camera to give a panoramic view of the Sea of Tranquillity panning slowly and picking out small craters. He then pointed it towards the sun. A long piece of angular rock could be seen in the distance. It was about 18 inches long.

There was then a shot of the shadow of the module and beyond that there were two craters. Armstrong said they were about 40 ft. long and about 20 ft. across.

Armstrong then swung the camera round again towards the lunar module and Aldrin could be seen erecting the solar wind instruments. Armstrong then left the TV camera on its tripod and moved into view, walking slowly towards Aldrin. By this time Armstrong had been on the lunar surface about 70 minutes, Aldrin somewhat less.

The two astronauts then began a thorough inspection of the lunar module to check whether there had been any damage to the struts on landing or any other exterior damage. They could be heard talking to each other by radio as they checked their fragile lunar aircraft.

As they then prepared to collect a larger sample of the moon dust and rocks, the voice of Michael Collins could be heard reporting to mission control as he came round from behind the moon, having completed an orbit in the mother ship, Columbia.

The two astronauts told him that they were just erecting the American flag, the Stars and Stripes, and Collins

> "For every American it must be the proudest moment of their lives, perhaps for everyone in the world."

replied: "Gee, that's great." The flag was planted at 4.41 A.M.

It seemed at first that Armstrong and Aldrin were having difficulty in getting the staff of the flag into the ground, but after a few minutes it was standing securely. One of the astronauts was then photographed standing by the side of the flag.

Aldrin could then be seen loping across the surface and guffaws of laughter from mission control were heard in the background. The astronaut began performing high jinks as he bounced up and down like a jack-in-the-box and leaping around in front of Eagle. The changed time for the moon walk has no bearing on the planned lift off, still set for 6.50 P.M. (B.S.T.) tonight.

Armstrong and Aldrin were then told to stand by to receive a message from President Nixon. The President told them that he was speaking from the White House by telephone and "this certainly has to be the most historic telephone call ever made." He said he wanted to tell them how proud everyone was. For every American it must be the proudest moment of their lives, perhaps for everyone in the world.

In a Troubled Time, the Moon Landing Restores Americans' Optimism

Andrea Billups

On the fortieth anniversary of the Apollo 11 moon landing, a journalist reports on the Navy frogman who opened the hatch of the returned spacecraft when it splashed down in the ocean. The sailor recalls how honored he felt to be the first to greet the astronauts and how happy he and others were about the moon landing, which came at a time when the United States was in turmoil over the assassinations of Martin Luther King, Jr. and John F. and Robert Kennedy and the Vietnam War. The moon landing made people believe Americans could accomplish something wonderful in spite of all the trouble. Those who participated in the space program cherish their memories of it, the article says, and like many others they hope that humans will return to the moon and go beyond. Andrea Billups is a former national features correspondent of the *Washington Times*, covering politics and culture.

The Apollo 11 crew is welcomed in New York City with a parade. Coming during a divisive war in Vietnam and after assassinations of several national leaders, the moon landing revived a sense of national pride. (NASA/ Newsmakers/Getty Images.)

Frogman Clancy Hatleberg waited on the ocean in the dark. It was July [of 1969] in the South Pacific, 400 miles southwest of Wake Island, and the waves were chopping hard.

Even as the weather was dicey, all eyes focused on the sky. It was the final leg of a nervous mission, and the recovery crew was focused on getting every detail right. Lives depended on it.

The world was watching.

Then they saw it, the Apollo 11 spacecraft, descending to Earth in a breathtaking finale, the capstone of a space program and a glorious achievement for a nation.

It was a beautiful sight, a big circle of huge clouds and below it darkness with the sun rising, caught between

night and day. And then in the middle of this big opening comes this fiery comet through the sky. The parachutes opened. . . . And then he snapped to, having drilled and drilled for this moment as he prepared to jump into the water and secure the craft and his own place in history.

Mr. Hatleberg, then 24, was an integral part of NASA's recovery effort, but he lauds the countless others who made that moment seem so effortless. In today's Navy, he would be called a SEAL, but back in 1969, he was a frogman diver who had honed his skills in Vietnam and was honored to be the first man who would greet Neil Armstrong, Buzz Aldrin and Michael Collins as they splashed down on July 24, 1969, after an eight-day mission that crystallized America's confidence and captured the admiration—and envy—of the world.

> It was a huge leap for a nation roiling in discord.

"It was stunning, absolutely," recalls Mr. Hatleberg, now a program manager for Apogen Technologies in San Diego.

He was the man who opened the spacecraft's hatch, handed the astronauts decontamination suits, sprayed them down with disinfectant and hoisted them into a life raft on their way back to the USS *Hornet* and an adoring throng. They had gone to the moon, an unfathomable feat, and yet it had happened, in an era sorely in need of some joy.

"I'm humbled by the experience, but the astronauts are the real heroes in this story," Mr. Hatleberg says. "They went into harm's way and risked their lives to take this giant leap."

Indeed, it was a huge leap for a nation roiling in discord. The civil rights movement had torn its brothers and sisters apart in racial angst. The Vietnam War was raging with antiwar protesters angling for a stop to what they deemed as senseless killing in faraway jungles. It may have been the dawning of the Age of Aquarius, but its actors were miles away from peace and love.

"We were angry about the war," remembers Mike Foley, who was a journalism student at the University of Florida when the Apollo 11 crew made that trip to the moon.

"It was a very aroused and aware time. I don't think we were innocent at all. I think we were [ticked] off."

> 'It was a moment that brought us all together at a time when we badly needed something to believe in.'

Mr. Foley, who went on to become editor of the *St. Petersburg Times* and is now an assistant dean and professor at Florida, was having homemade pizza with a group of married students in Gainesville, Fla., the night of the historic moonwalk. He remembers all of his group walking out, like so many others across the nation, and gazing at the summer's night sky, looking at the moon and imagining that such a powerful feat was happening. "You couldn't see anything," he says, laughing, "but just to know it was going on was humbling."

"I think everyone was transfixed. They couldn't believe that men were actually walking on the moon," says Mr. Foley, who watched the two-hour, 31-minute moonwalk on television with his friends.

"We had been in the space race, and I think it caused such a panic with Sputnik and that Russia was ahead of us. And we had finally made it," he recalls. "I think it was a moment that brought us all together at a time when we badly needed something to believe in."

"Looking back," Mr. Foley says, "the moon trip seems so insignificant now. We had no cell phones, no computers. They essentially took a Model T up there in terms of rocketry, and it worked! It's miraculous."

The Apollo program began with the dreams of President John F. Kennedy, who embraced a goal of landing on the moon by the end of the '60s.

"I believe that this nation should commit itself to achieving the goal, before this decade is out, of landing a man on the moon and returning him safely to the Earth. No single space project in this period will be more impressive to mankind, or more important for the long-range exploration of space; and none will be so difficult or expensive to accomplish," Mr. Kennedy declared on May 25, 1961, in a special message to Congress.

Although Mr. Kennedy did not live to see it materialize, by the time the Apollo era ended, the early space program included multiple uncrewed test missions and 11 space trips carrying astronauts. Six of those missions—11, 12, 14, 15, 16 and 17—included landing on the moon, according to NASA history.

Before the historic Apollo 11 lunar walk, earlier Apollo journeys tested the command and lunar modules, dubbed Columbia and Eagle respectively, that eventually brought the Apollo 11 crew safely to the moon's surface on the now-famous Sea of Tranquility.

The breathtaking maiden moon visit lasted for just 21.6 hours, but many who watched an astronaut plod down the steps of the lunar module in a cumbersome white spacesuit felt as though the moment had lasted a lifetime as they braced in front of televisions to see what might happen as he made his first tenuous steps on the dusty surface.

> By the time Mr. Armstrong put his craft down, they had just 20 seconds of fuel left.

"The unknowns were rampant," Mr. Armstrong would say later. "There were just a thousand things to worry about."

By the time Mr. Armstrong put his craft down, they had just 20 seconds of fuel left. "Houston, Tranquility Base here. The Eagle has landed," the commander radioed as NASA control and the nation waited, breathless.

"Roger, Tranquility," the controller said back. "We copy you to the ground."

He later added, conveying the Mission Control's relief after an unnerving moment: "You got a bunch of guys about to turn blue. We're breathing again."

Mr. Armstrong and Mr. Aldrin, in a little-known detail, actually ate their first meal before stepping out to explore a place where no one had walked before. While on the moon, they conducted experiments and gathered 46 pounds of lunar rocks and soil for study back at home.

"It was more than one small step for man, as Mr. Armstrong famously dubbed it over the crackling airways, but an astounding feat that has yet to be replicated," says Bob Fish, curator of the USS Hornet Museum in Alameda Point, Calif., on the San Francisco Bay. There, members of the recovery crew will gather for a 40th anniversary celebration, with Mr. Aldrin paying a visit to greet the still-admiring throngs.

"I remember the Cuban missile crisis well," says Mr. Fish, a Marine who worked in strategic defense communications and volunteered as an Apollo curator. He wrote the book *Hornet Plus Three: The Story of the Apollo 11 Recovery.*

"I was 14, and I remember B-52 bombers launched from McCoy Air Force Base in Orlando [Florida] rattling like an earthquake. I was sure it was over with. We were sure we were dead. Then Kennedy was assassinated and the Vietnam War came and then Martin Luther King was shot. It was just awful, chaos and turmoil.

And then, from the ashes of our mess, rose this beautiful thing. It makes me tear up a little bit when I think about us going to the moon. We did it! We showed, instead of being this chaotic society, we proved to the world that out of it could come these fantastic scientific achievements like walking on the moon."

Milt Putnam, a retired photojournalist living in North Carolina, carries the images of the space era close. Now 74, he was chosen as the Navy's top photographer to capture, alongside a NASA shooter, three recovery missions, including Apollo 11. It was his photographs that were transmitted around the world, including a now-famous shot of President [Richard] Nixon greeting the isolation trailer on the USS *Hornet* as the Apollo 11 crew laughed and waved inside their quarantine chamber.

Mr. Nixon later asked Mr. Putnam for copies of his shots, and the photographer received a thank-you note from the commander in chief lauding his effort.

Not that it was easy. Mr. Putnam recalls practicing and preparing for every eventuality, making practice runs to take notes on lighting and weather conditions, and making pictures strapped onto the side of a helicopter. There was little room for error with a 30- to 40-minute shooting window. He was to capture a moment that could not be re-created.

He did not sleep much the previous night, rising at 3 A.M. to dine and get in place for a 5:50 A.M. local-time splashdown. He carried eight Nikon cameras and 75 rolls of black-and-white and color film. It was long before the days of auto-focus and digital capabilities.

Once strapped in, with Apollo 11 streaming in on radar, the pilot lowered the hatch door on the helicopter. Mr. Putnam's light meter caught on the cable and snapped, falling into the ocean. I hope it's not whale bait, he joked nervously.

And then it was showtime, no time for nerves but all business. "It hit me while I was shooting, that these guys just came back from the moon," Mr. Putnam said. "I had a feeling come over me, but I couldn't just sit there and contemplate. I was emotional, but I had to keep shooting and get everything I could."

"My heart was still pumping at the end of the day," he says of his role in history. "I was very proud. It was a big honor for a little boy from a South Carolina mill town."

Today, 40 years later, many in the country remain hopeful that we can once again return to the moon and beyond, including Mr. Putnam.

> It was a mankind moment, greater than any one human, than any society.

"I'm disappointed because we had come so far in such a short time. I don't regret the space shuttle because it was needed, but if this country had continued, we would already be on Mars. You just know that our astronauts are ready to go."

On the 40th anniversary of the first moon landing, many in the country remain hopeful that the nation can once again return to the moon and farther out, with new missions looking toward visits to Mars.

President [Barack] Obama has said he is committed to U.S. goals of returning to the moon[1] and beyond, and has reviewed the current NASA budget, which is strained amid the sliding economy as resources are needed to take care of issues at home.

Mr. Obama also has named retired Marine Corps Maj. Gen. Charles F. Bolden Jr., a former space shuttle astronaut, to head the National Aeronautics and Space Administration.

Those who participated in the space program remain confident that someday it will be restored. Until then, their memories of an era sustain them.

"It's kind of hard if you haven't lived through it, but this was our generation's 9-11 moment," Mr. Fish said, referencing the Sept. 11 [2001] terrorist attacks.

"Those who lived through it remember where they were and what they were doing when we landed a man on the moon. It was one of those watershed moments in the psyche of the nation."

"If there had been Twitter then, it would have been completely overwhelmed," he said. "It was a mankind moment, greater than any one human, than any society. The whole world looked at the moon at that moment. And we were bigger than anything here on Earth."

Note

1. As of 2010, President Obama had decided against returning to the moon in favor of preparation for eventual trips to the asteroids and Mars.

Apollo 11's Greatest Significance Lies in the Knowledge Gained by Humankind

Robert Hotz

The week after the moon landing, *Aviation Week & Space Technology*, a major magazine of the aerospace field, published the following editorial on why Apollo 11 was so significant. Robert Hotz, who was then the magazine's editor in chief, declares that all past theories about other worlds, both of science and of science fiction, will become obsolete because of the new knowledge provided by exploration of the moon. Also, he says, the Apollo 11 mission demonstrated that it is better to show space achievements to the world instead of keeping them secret, and that management of space programs by engineers is more successful than control by scientists, as was done by the Soviet Union. He argues that future human survival may ultimately depend on space technology if Earth becomes uninhabitable, and that Apollo 11 has provided proof that a new environment could be sought.

The small step of Neil Armstrong's boot from the lower rung of the lunar module landing gear ladder to the powdery surface of the moon was indeed a giant leap for all mankind.

Man's first adventure on the lurain [lunar terrain] embodied many triumphs of technology and spirit. But its greatest significance will prove to be the watershed it marks in man's knowledge of himself and his universe. From now on, the theories that have beguiled scientists and fiction writers alike will fade swiftly into obscurity as they are submerged by the vast quantity of new facts garnered in man's accelerating exploration of the moon and the rest of his universe.

Vanished already are the horror stories of man's difficulties in operating on the moon—banished by the swift mobility, varied work and easy communications of Neil Armstrong and "Buzz" Aldrin in man's initial 2 hr. on the lurain. Gone too are the long-espoused theories on deep layers of lunar dust that would engulf both man and spacecraft—refuted by the first scuffs of man's boots and the hard, mallet-driven progress of the core-sampling drill. Going fast are many of the theories of a cold, dead moon—jolted by Armstrong and Aldrin's first observations of lunar rocks. The first 78-lb. load of rocks brought back by the Eagle crew from Tranquility base will provide more answers on the origin and composition of the moon than a century of stargazing through instruments from earth.

Less than a week after the Apollo 11 crew returned safely to earth, the Mariner satellites will start transmitting back to earth man's first close view of the Martian surface in another astonishing triumph of space age science fact over theoretical fiction.

THE PUBLIC'S VIEW OF THE MOON LANDING

This is how Americans responded to a 1999 Gallup poll published on the thirtieth anniversary of the Apollo 11 moon landing.

	Yes	No	No opinion
Has the space program brought enough benefits to this country to justify the cost?	55%	40%	5%
Would you say the human race accomplished its single greatest technological achievement of all time by landing a man on the moon?	39%	59%	2%
Did you watch the first moon landing on television? (Based on people over 5 years old in 1969)	76%	21%	3%
Do you think the government staged or faked the moon landing?	6%	89%	5%

	Correct	Incorrect	No opinion
How many men have walked on the moon? (Correct answer: 12)	5%	88%	7%
Who was the first person to walk on the moon? (Correct answer: Neil Armstrong)	50%	22%	28%

Taken from: Data from Gallup News Service, July 20, 1999. www.gallup.com/poll/3712/landing-man-moon-publics-view.aspx.

Among the other triumphs of Apollo 11 that should be noted are:

Open Program over Secrecy

The U.S. policy of an open space program for all the world to see paid a stupendous dividend on Apollo 11 as people of almost every nation on earth were able to see man's first steps on the moon in that incredible television transmission. Never has the American image been projected brighter on such a global scale. It showed all mankind that this country is truly willing to share its triumphs, tragedies and knowledge will all who care to participate. The world owes a great debt to Stanley Lebar and his Westinghouse colleagues, who conceived and built the tiny 7-lb. television camera that transmitted so faithfully from the moon, and also to the National Aeronautics and Space Administration officials, who fought so hard to keep it on the mission.

> " The U.S. policy of an open space program for all the world to see paid a stupendous dividend on Apollo 11. "

Engineers over Scientists

One of the key differences between the U.S. and USSR space programs has been the divergent philosophies of its managers. The USSR program, dominated by the senior scientists of the powerful Academy of Sciences, has tended to overestimate the technical problems of manned spaceflight and insisted on over-testing with un-manned spacecraft or animal subjects. The U.S. program is managed by engineers backed by experience with operational development of high-speed aircraft from the X-1 to X-15. They have tackled problems such as the sound, heat and bio-medical barriers by designing and procuring around them, while U.S. ground-bound sci-entist experts in these fields urged slowdowns or aban-doning manned space flight. The engineering approach not only enabled the U.S. to overtake and pass the USSR

Stanley Lebar's versatile camera made it possible for the world to watch as humanity first set foot on another celestial body. (**AP Images.**)

in the race to put men on the moon, but is also producing far more scientific data faster than the conservative small-step programs of the scientist-dominated USSR effort. The wild gyrations of Luna 15 in lunar orbit and its ignominious crash in the Sea of Crises at the same time Astronauts Armstrong and Aldrin were broadcasting priceless data from the Sea of Tranquility offered a valid contrast in the two national philosophies.

Manned over Unmanned Spacecraft

Apollo 11 was another demonstration of the vital necessity for man in the control loop for a truly effective space exploration vehicle. Without man aboard, the lunar module would have crashed in an uncharted crater of huge boulders. Wailing would have been heard around the world on the futility of trying to land spacecraft on the lurain. With Neil Armstrong at the controls, the danger of the automatic landing site was quickly recognized. Eagle was flown manually beyond the dangerous crater to a feathery touchdown on powdery sand. In addition, the LM [lunar module] guidance computer became overloaded, rebelled and flashed false alarms until it was bypassed by the human brains aboard. No unmanned spacecraft could have accomplished the reconnaissance, evaluation and experimenting that Armstrong and Aldrin did in their relatively short lunar stay. Unmanned spacecraft are certainly necessary for preliminary exploration of distant planets just as Ranger, Surveyor and Orbiter blazed a trail for Apollo. But man must eventually be on board to insure the mission's operational and scientific success.

> "Apollo 11 also gives man his first spark of immortality. It demonstrated that he no longer need be a prisoner of his earthly home."

Apollo 11 also gives man his first spark of immortality. It demonstrated that he no longer need be a prisoner of his earthly home. If, at some future time, this planet becomes uninhabitable because of a nuclear war, cumulative pollution or the end of its galactic cycle, the human race now has the capacity to seek a new environment.

Man may find that his ultimate survival as a species may depend solely on his resources of space technology and his skill as a space voyager.

CHAPTER 2

Controversies Surrounding the Apollo 11 Moon Landing

Landing on the Moon Is Important to the Future of Humanity

Margaret Mead

In an article written shortly before the moon landing, a prominent anthropologist observes that some people are already questioning its meaning and retreating from the wider view of the universe space travel offers. She argues that this is because of what has been called "future shock" and that the situation is similar to that of the fifteenth century, when explorers made voyages of discovery, not solving any immediate problems by doing so, but ultimately transforming the world. The urge to explore is crucial to humanity, she says, and only through new experiences can humans gain the knowledge and skills required to deal with worldwide problems on Earth. Margaret Mead wrote many popular books and articles as well as scholarly works on cultural anthropology. She was awarded the Presidential Medal of Freedom posthumously for her work in bringing concepts from her academic field to the public at large.

Photo on previous page: Some Apollo opponents say its funds should have gone toward problems on Earth; a few people suggest that men never walked on the moon. (**Space Frontiers/ Getty Images.**)

Thee day a man steps onto the surface of the moon, human beings will be taking a decisive step out of the past into a new reality.

Long ago our ancestors lived on very small islands of the known, scattered on an unknown planet. The whole of a universe could be encompassed in a hilltop and a valley, the steady stars, the wandering Pleiades and the waxing and waning moon. Mountain walls, vast plains, dark forests and the fringing seas cut off little groups of men from knowledge of what lay beyond their own familiar patch of earth, and the arching sky was accessible to them only in fantasy.

Today the deeply important thing is that the same set of inventions that is opening the universe to exploration also has made our world one, a bounded unit within which all human beings share the same hazards and have access to the same hopes. This is why I think the moon landing is a momentous event.

But as we wait for the astronaut to take that first step onto a part of the solar system that is not our earth, it seems to me that our vision is faltering. We have followed each stage of this venture into space. Through the camera's eye we have already looked down at barren stretches of moonscape and we have seen our own world, a small, shining globe in space. But as the first climax approaches, wonder at the unknown and a sense of the magnificence of the achievement are dimmed and tarnished by doubt and the feeling on the part of many people that "all this is meaningless to me."

Why Go to the Moon?

The same questions have been asked for a decade. Why go to the moon? Why spend all that money on a space program that will change no one's daily life and solve none of the problems of human misery on earth? Can't we put the same money to much better use here? Why not put the earth in order before we take off into space?

Photo on previous page: "A society that no longer moves forward," wrote anthropologist Margaret Mead, "begins to die." (Archive Photos/ Getty Images.)

Who cares whether we or the Russians win this "race"? With the danger of nuclear warfare and the menace of uncontrolled population growth—both the outcome of modern science—confronting us, why should anyone get excited about one more technological success, the landing of a man on the moon?

> Many people are shrinking from the future and from participation in the movement toward a new, expanded reality. And like homesick travelers abroad, they are focusing their anxieties on home.

These are the wrong questions to be asking, I think. They are evidence, it seems to me, that we are suffering from a failure of the imagination, a failure of nerve, that psychiatrists are beginning to recognize as *future shock*. It is well known that people who go to live in a strange place among strangers whose language and manners are incomprehensible often suffer from culture shock, a state of mind in which, alienated and homesick, they temporarily lose their ability to take in new experience. In somewhat the same way many people are shrinking from the future and from participation in the movement toward a new, expanded reality. And like homesick travelers abroad, they are focusing their anxieties on home.

The reasons are not far to seek. We are at a turning point in human history. What is required of us is not merely a change in our conceptions, but also in our sense of scale. The only parallel to the situation with which we are confronted lies five hundred years in our past, just before the great era of world exploration.

A Parallel from History

Then, in the 1420's, Prince Henry—an extraordinary technologist whom we only vaguely remember as "Henry the Navigator," brother of the king of Portugal—gathered around him a great company of scholars, astronomers, map makers, pilots, instrument makers and craftsmen in Sagres, on a lonely promontory reaching out into the unexplored Atlantic. They created a new science of navigation and invented a new kind of ship, the lateen-rigged caravel, which could make headway against the winds and was designed for long sea voyages. Up to that time ships navigated from island to island or from point to point, close to shore; where this was impossible, few men sailed intentionally.

For forty years Prince Henry sent ship after ship into the Atlantic and down the coast of Africa, hoping to solve the "impossible" problem of circling the continent. His were not the first craft to reach the nearer islands or to attempt the African voyage or even to rove the open Atlantic. But the men who sailed the caravels were the first to study and plot systematically the winds and currents off the African coast and, eventually, on the open seas from the North to the South Atlantic. And it was from seamen trained in Sagres, only a few years after Prince Henry's death, that [Christopher] Columbus learned his seamanship.

> We could turn our attention to the problems that going to the moon certainly will not solve. . . . But I think this would be fatal to our future.

Prince Henry and his company of scientists and technicians formed one of the small clusters of men whose work began the transformation of the world. They solved no immediate problems. The Moors, against whom Henry fought as a young man, still were a threat to Mediterranean Europe when he died. The Portuguese inventions made feasible long voyages of discovery, but no one knew what lay ahead. And certainly no one could foresee that the greatest innovation was the new approach to problem solution, which combined theory and the deliberate creation of a technology to carry out practical experiments. Only today do we fully realize that this linkage of science and technology in the thinking of Prince

Henry and others of his time made possible a world in which people could believe in and work toward progress.

The parallel, of course, is an imperfect one. Where it breaks down most seriously is in the number of people involved. In the fifteenth century only a handful of men were aware of the tremendous breakthrough in knowledge. Today in an intercommunicating world, millions of people enter into the debate and are part of the decision-making process that will determine how we shall deal with the knowledge, the anxieties and the hopes that are part of this contemporary expansion of reality. And it is extraordinarily difficult for vast numbers of people to move simultaneously toward change.

The Need to Explore

We could slow down and wait. We could turn our attention to the problems that going to the moon certainly will not solve. We could hope that, given time, more men would become aware of new possibilities. But I think this would be fatal to our future.

As I see it, this new exploration—this work at the edge of human knowledge—is what will keep us human. It will keep us from turning backward toward ways of thinking and acting that have separated men from their full humanity. For humanity is not to be found by going back to some Golden Age when communities were small and the people living in them knew and trusted (but also, in reality, often bitterly hated and despised) one another. Humanity is not to be found in any kind of romantic retreat, in any denial of present reality, in any decision to rest within the known.

Humanity lies in man's urge to explore the world. It lies in man's unique drive to understand the nature of the universe within which he lives. It lies in man's capacity to question the known and imagine the unknown.

Step by difficult step men expanded the world they knew to include the whole of the planet and all men living on it. In the seventeenth century, men's conception of the universe was transformed by the telescope, which brought the moon and the stars nearer, and by the microscope, through which the once-indecipherable nature of matter was made intelligible. Once men could count only the smallest collections of objects, and until our own generation the organization of vast assemblages of facts was an infinitely laborious task. Today the use of computers allows men to think about organized complexity on a scale entirely new. And now, finally, we are moving out from the earth as living beings, in the persons of the astronauts, to experience space with all our capacities, our wonder and thirst for understanding. For the first time we are exercising in full reality what has been truly called man's cosmic sense.

> A society that no longer moves forward does not merely stagnate; it begins to die.

Each stage of discovery has enlarged not only men's understanding of the world, but also their awareness of human potentialities. So I believe we cannot stop now on the threshold of new experience. We must put our knowledge to the test. Human potentialities, unexercised, can wither and fester, can become malignant and dangerous. A society that no longer moves forward does not merely stagnate; it begins to die.

New Ways to Solve Problems

The exploration of space does not mean neglect of the tremendously difficult problems of our immediate environment. It will mean, I think, the development of a new context within which we can look for viable solutions. Up to now, our ideas about what can be done have been either utopian or essentially parochial, while the problems themselves affect the well-being of human beings everywhere.

It is no accident that the Soviet Union and the United States, the two largest organized modern states, have

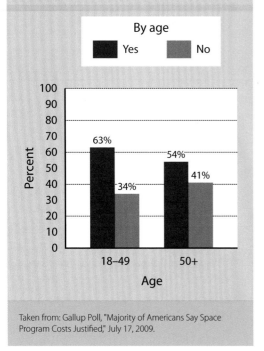

MAJORITY OF AMERICANS SAY SPACE PROGRAM COSTS JUSTIFIED

It is now forty years since the United States first landed men on the moon. Do you think the space program has brought enough benefits to this country to justify its costs?

By age

■ Yes   ■ No

63%
54%
41%
34%

18–49   50+

Age

Percent

Taken from: Gallup Poll, "Majority of Americans Say Space Program Costs Justified," July 17, 2009.

built and launched the first successful spacecraft, while the governments of the 180 million people in the Common Market countries of western Europe [Belgium, France, Germany, Italy, Luxembourg, and the Netherlands] have continued to bicker divisively and ineffectually over which stage of a shared rocket should be built by whom and have been unable to find ways of co-ordinating their efforts. Nor is it an accident that these two countries are moving ahead so fast in changing and raising the level of education—though in this we still, by far, lead the world.

In part the success of the Soviet Union and the United States has resulted from the fact that these two countries have—and have been willing to commit—the resources in money and men and organization necessary for so large-scale an enterprise. In part it is owing to their orientation to the future. Soviet and American men and women have no monopoly on talent. But each of us, as a country, has been able to attain the precise and magnificent large-scale co-ordination of effort necessary for building spacecraft and for becoming pioneers in the space age.

The very thing that has made the space program successful, but also in the eyes of many people boring, is awareness of the crucial importance of detail. The rehearsals, the repetitiveness, the careful steps, the determination on absolute precautions and the participation of the citizenry in something that might, but must not, go wrong—all these things also are essential to the success of an enterprise on a new, unprecedented scale.

No country, as yet, has fully recognized the fact that the scale of our major human problems is not local or national but regional or world-wide. No country has realized that we must simultaneously include both extremes—the individual and all men—in working toward social solutions. Individual human dignity can be assured only when all men everywhere are accorded and accord to others their full humanity. National solutions are inadequate as they are based on past conceptions of human differences, uneconomic uses of resources and barriers to communication that no longer exist.

We have yet to discover how to co-ordinate effort to solve social problems on the scale that will be necessary. This will mean, as it has in the space program, work with small models, new kinds of simulations and trials and intensive learning before we move into large new systems of organization with planetary repercussions. No more than the fifteenth-century men who opened the seas to exploration can we see what lies ahead. But unlike the early explorers, we have learned how to direct our efforts.

The lunar landing will be a triumph in its own right. But at the same time nothing can demonstrate more cogently, I feel, that there is an intimate and inescapable connection between man's pursuit of his destiny and his attainment of his own humanity than the intricate technological co-ordination combined with individual human courage that characterizes both the American and the Soviet space programs. There is no reason for alienation from experience that will enhance our common humanity. Voyages to the moon—and beyond the moon—are one assurance of our ability to live on the earth.

The Apollo Moon Landing Was a Senseless Waste of Effort

Gerard J. DeGroot

In the following viewpoint, a historian contends that the public did not seriously consider the purpose of landing on the moon, implying that if they had, they would have seen little meaning in it. He agrees with the civil rights activists who protested spending money on space instead of social problems, and he does not feel that the space race with the Soviets had a significant effect on the outcome of the Cold War. Furthermore, he does not see any validity in the belief that going to another world was a momentous step in human evolution. In his opinion, the strongly favorable public reaction to Apollo 11 was mere romanticism. Gerard DeGroot is a professor of history at the University of St. Andrews in Scotland.

SOURCE. Gerard J. DeGroot, "Chapter 13: Magnificent Desolation," *Dark Side of the Moon: The Magnificent Madness of the American Lunar Quest.* New York University Press, 2006, pp. 233–243. Copyright © 2006 by New York University Press. All rights reserved. Reproduced by permission.

The manner in which the space race had been conducted ensured that it was never allowed to be anything other than a race. In order to attain top speed the Americans had stripped away from their space program all the cumbersome scientific and emotional baggage that might otherwise have given it purpose and meaning. Apollo was lean but empty. [Astronaut Neil] Armstrong admitted as much in a press conference on July 5 [1969]. "The objective of this flight is precisely to take man to the Moon, make a landing there and return," he said. "The primary objective is the ability to demonstrate that man, in fact, can do this kind of job."

Opposition from Civil Rights Activists

Space was a dominating issue of the 1960s; civil rights was another. The two were distinctly separate: space showcased the country's achievement; civil rights underlined her shortcomings. The two issues did nevertheless intersect, most often when civil rights campaigners argued that the billions required to put a few men into orbit could be better utilized to help millions of blacks onto their feet. On the eve of the *Apollo 11* launch, the activist Ralph Abernathy argued that:

> A society that can resolve to conquer space . . . deserves acclaim for achievement and contempt for bizarre social values. For though it has had the capacity to meet extraordinary challenges, it has failed to use its ability to rid itself of the scourges of racism, poverty and war, all of which were brutally scarring the nation even as it mobilized for the assault on the solar system. . . . Why is it less exciting to the human spirit to enlarge man by making him brother to his fellow man? There is more distance between the races of man than between the moon and the earth. To span the vastness of human space is ultimately more glorious than any other achievement.

Members of the Poor People's Campaign, seen here marching near the Cape Kennedy space complex, were among many who protested the Apollo program's expense. (**AP Images.**)

Abernathy's complaint reached a crescendo when he led a march of perhaps three hundred followers from the Poor People's Campaign to the *Apollo 11* launch site. A light rain was falling as his army approached. A number of mules, symbols of rural poverty, were in the van, providing a stark contrast to the massive, high-tech Saturn rocket. Abernathy stopped, then gave a short speech to a crowd of onlookers who had the Moon on their mind. He pointed out that one-fifth of the nation lacked adequate food, clothing, shelter, and medical care and that, given such deep poverty, space flight seemed inhumane. The crowd remained polite, but most of the spectators wanted this spoil-sport to get out of the way so that the show could start.

Abernathy was met by Tom Paine [NASA's administrator] who had by his side, appropriately, Julian Scheer, NASA's public information officer. Paine's presence was carefully engineered to suggest that NASA took the plight of the poor seriously, even if it could do nothing to alleviate that suffering. He explained that he was himself a member of the NAACP and sensitive to the struggle of poor blacks. But he told Abernathy (and the assembled crowd) "if we could solve the problems of poverty by not pushing the button to launch men to the Moon tomorrow, then we would not push that button." He called the task of exploring space mere "child's play" compared to "the tremendously difficult human problems" that concerned Abernathy and other social activists. As trite as that sounded, it was probably true. Then, in a clever bit of manipulation, he asked Abernathy to pray for the safety of the astronauts. Abernathy could hardly refuse. In the end, the protest had as much thrust as a Vanguard rocket [only three out of eleven Vanguard launches attempted from 1957 to 1959 successfully placed satellites into orbit].

Paine offered to admit a delegation from Abernathy's campaign to view the launch from within the area reserved for special guests. Buses were dispatched to Cocoa to pick up the group, with food packets provided. In all, one hundred men, women, and children from the campaign were admitted as honored guests of NASA. The space agency had once again worked its magic. Interviewed about the launch, Abernathy, against his better instincts, was briefly overcome by emotion. He concluded, "I'm happy that we're going to the Moon; but I'd be even happier if we had learned to live together here on Earth."

Meaningless Space Race

"Go baby, go!" [TV news anchor] Walter Cronkite hollered as the Saturn V rose from the pad on July 16. The journey to the Moon had become routine, given the success of the three previous Apollo missions. The only remaining uncertainty was the actual landing, something that could not really be practiced without actually doing it. . . .

Meanwhile, the unmanned Soviet *Luna 15* craft passed overhead. It had been launched three days before *Apollo 11* and had been in lunar orbit during the Americans' approach. It appears that the Soviets intended to land on the Moon, grab a soil sample, then quickly blast off, beating the Americans back to Earth. This would allow them to claim that they had landed on the Moon first and were first to bring back samples. If that was indeed the intention, it is an interesting comment on the ridiculous nature of the space race, and the obsession with making human beings the principal runners. The Soviets started that race with Laika the wonder dog [the first dog in space], but were defeated by that same obsession. How ironic, then, that they tried, at the last resort, to cheat on rules they themselves had written. In fact, *Luna* (and irony) crashed into the Sea of Crises.

> How precisely the lunar landing demonstrated the superiority of democracy was not clear. But as a demonstration of capitalism it was brilliant.

Back home, the cosmonauts [members of the Russian space program] thanked the stars for their lucky escape.

[Dave] Scott, like so many of the astronauts steeped in the politics of the space race, believes that the lunar landing was an important victory in the Cold War.

"[President John F.] Kennedy's deadline had been met. We'd beaten the Russians. As Kennedy had said, it was the Soviet Union that had chosen space as the arena to demonstrate the superiority of its system. But we had shown them our system was better." As [President Dwight D.] Eisenhower had once argued, there were probably easier, cheaper, and more meaningful ways to make that point.

The "system" was capitalism and democracy. How precisely the lunar landing demonstrated the superiority of democracy was not clear. But as a demonstration of capitalism it was brilliant. In July 1969, it was virtually impossible to find an advertisement that did not mention the lunar landing. While NASA was careful not to be seen to be endorsing any product, it did not object when advertisers used space themes to peddle soft drinks, alcohol, cigarettes, candy, cars, airlines, panty hose, perfume and hundreds of other products. Photos of the Moon and of NASA equipment were usually provided free of charge. One of the best ads had a faithful reconstruction of the *Apollo 11* module on the lunar surface. Armstrong emerged to find the Frito Bandito had beaten him to the Moon. "Welcome to the Moon, Señor!"

Banal Media Coverage

Television coverage of the event was like a king-size blanket bought at K-Mart: huge, but awfully thin. CBS alone deployed 142 cameras and a crew in excess of one thousand in order to broadcast banalities to the nation. The networks competed with one another in the "expert" opinion they mobilized. Each had at least one retired astronaut. There were also poets (James Dickey and Marianne Moore), media personalities (Steve Allen, Barbara Walters, and Joe Garagiola), musicians (Duke Ellington premiered his "Moon Maiden"), scientists (Robert Jastrow and Harold Urey), and a wide assortment of other commentators (Marshall McLuhan, Rod McKuen,

Arthur C. Clarke, Orson Welles, Ray Bradbury, Margaret Mead). The whole affair was like an arms race transferred to television: network producers had far more weapons than they could ever possibly use. Those who suffered were the scientists, since no one wanted unintelligible science to ruin a good story. "The producers didn't seem to have too much understanding of the science of the event," one astrophysicist complained.

> No one wanted to tackle the big questions: Why precisely did America go to the Moon, what benefits might accrue, what, realistically, might the United States do next?

Writing in the *New Statesman*, [British journalist] James Cameron remarked ironically on how newsmen used to be criticized for sensationalizing small events. Yet here was a big event which they had "reduce[d] . . . intuitively to a sort of basic piffle . . . a level of numbing vitality." No one wanted to tackle the big questions: Why precisely did America go to the Moon, what benefits might accrue, what, realistically, might the United States do next, what did the whole thing say about America? "It could have been an elevating and eventually a self-revealing week in the history of man's lurching attempts to understand his world and himself," wrote *Newsweek* journalist Edwin Diamond. "But no one had the time or the inclination to approach meaningful material in a fresh way, to seriously consider, for example, the proposition: "We go to the Moon because we want to, we don't fix the urban mess because we don't want to."

It was precisely because journalists had, for nearly a decade, faithfully followed the NASA script that the whole lunar enterprise had gone forward without serious questioning. Few critics had the guts to ask the difficult questions; those who did were dismissed as unpatriotic or Luddite by the NASA press corps. Cronkite derisively referred to the few doubters as "left-wing opposition." "I wonder what all those . . . who pooh-poohed this program are saying now," he remarked moments after the lunar landing. NASA's gratitude was expressed by [rocket engineer] Wernher von Braun, who told the press corps at the end of the mission: "I would like to thank all of you for all of the fine support you have always given the program, because without public relations and good presentations of these programs to the public, we would have been unable to do it."

Public Emotion

From July 19 to the 29th, the northeastern United States experienced virtually continuous rain. New York City had only five hours of sunshine during the entire period, flash floods hit Vermont, and the Cape Cod tourist board estimated losses at $250,000 per day. Some people blamed NASA. Quoting scripture, they argued that the bad weather was God's punishment for man's invasion of the heavens. But relief eventually came. "I've just seen the Sun on my porch for two minutes," a Bronx woman remarked when phoning a local weather station. "I think we're safe now. I thought sure, because we'd broken all the laws, that we'd never see the Sun again."

In contrast, the vast majority of people were delighted by news from the Moon. In the USSR, the cosmonauts realized they had lost the race, but were still sufficiently big-hearted to admire what had been achieved. "I wanted man to succeed in making it to the Moon," Alexei Leonov confessed. "If it couldn't be me, let it be this crew, I thought, with what we in Russia call 'white envy'—envy mixed with admiration." At the time of Neil Armstrong's small step, Leonov was at the Space Transmission Corps in Moscow, where the Americans' every move was closely monitored. "Even in the military center where I stood, where military men were observing the achievements of our rival superpower, there was loud applause."

Perhaps as many as one billion people around the world watched some portion of the mission on live television—the biggest audience in television history. Queen Elizabeth stayed up to watch the moon walk live. So, too, did the pope. According to the *New York Times*, the mission captured the imagination of people "from Wollongong, Australia, where a local judge brought in a television set to watch while hearing cases, to Norwegian Lapland, where shepherds tended their reindeer with transistors pressed to their ears." Trading halted on the Sydney Stock Exchange and crime rates in Milan fell by two-thirds. In Warsaw, one thousand cheering Poles packed the U.S. Embassy; in Kraków, a statue of the Apollo crew was unveiled. Across Europe, streets were deserted as crowds clustered around TV sets. The jamming of Voice of America transmissions in Cuba was briefly lifted so that the people could witness America triumphant. Everywhere, traveling Americans were stopped in the streets, congratulated, and offered free drinks. Michael Fisher, an eighteen-year-old American in Moscow on a Quaker-sponsored exchange that summer, "happened to walk by the U.S. embassy that day and encountered quite a few Russians standing on the sidewalk right outside, eager to congratulate any Americans they could find."

In Rome, at Christmas, a nativity scene in the Piazza Navona had a lunar module parked just behind the stable, while two astronauts, in full space gear and on bended knee, paid homage to the infant Christ. In Fife, Scotland, a boy born just after the lunar landing was named Neil Edwin Michael. Mrs. Delmar Moon of Toledo, Ohio, could not resist naming her son Neil Armstrong Moon. In Dacca, a baby Pakistani boy was named Apollo. Henry Mancini released a new arrangement of Beethoven's "Moonlight Sonata," to wide acclaim. . . .

> The magnitude of the event unleashed a torrent of romantic nonsense.

Romantic Nonsense

The magnitude of the event unleashed a torrent of romantic nonsense. In an article in *TV Guide* prior to the launch, Cronkite remarked: "When Apollo 11 reaches the Moon, when we reach that unreachable star, we will have shown that the possibility of world peace exists . . . if we put our skill, intelligence and money to it." Wernher von Braun, never one to resist hyperbole, called the lunar landing "equal in importance to that moment in evolution when aquatic life came crawling up on the land." [Noted engineer] Buckminster Fuller, echoing von Braun, put *Apollo 11* at the "dead center of evolutionary events," whatever that meant. [President] Richard Nixon, eager to get in on the act, called it "the greatest week in the history since the beginning of the world, the creation. Nothing has changed the world more than this mission." That remark deeply annoyed his friend [prominent religious leader] Billy Graham, who supplied, for good measure, three more important events: the birth of Christ, the crucifixion, and the first Easter.

> Contrary to all the illusions, a small step on the Moon did not erase mankind's propensity for cruelty.

"For one priceless moment in the whole history of man, all the people on this Earth are truly one," Nixon claimed. That was perhaps true, but it was just a moment. Like so many others, Nixon made the mistake of thinking that a popular spectacle was automatically an influential event. "It is the spirit of Apollo that America can now help to bring to our relations with other nations," he remarked to the American people with a crack in his voice. "The spirit of Apollo transcends geographical barriers and political differences. It can bring the people of the world together in peace." At that precise moment, Jews in Palestine were doing dreadful things to Arabs, and vice versa. Vietnam was witnessing the worst

> One of history's greatest ironies was that so much beauty and imagination was invested into a trip to a sterile rock of no purpose to anyone.

violence of its long war. Contrary to all the illusions, a small step on the Moon did not erase mankind's propensity for cruelty. In any case, Nixon seems to have forgotten that without Cold War mistrust there would never have been a lunar mission.

Armstrong encouraged those who wanted to believe in an epochal event. Nearly everyone knows what he said when he first stepped on the Moon: "That's one small step for man, one giant leap for mankind." . . .

People accepted that that one small step was a giant leap for mankind simply because Armstrong said it was so. Few paused to consider how walking around the Moon in a space suit brought progress to mankind. How exactly did it help the starving in Africa? To what extent did it help the Vietnamese peasants who were murdering each other for the sake of an arcane struggle between communism and capitalism? Did African Americans watching the landing in a fetid shack in Alabama suddenly shout: "Golly, my life is so much better because Neil took that small step!"? Some people obviously thought so.

Magnificent Desolation

Armstrong's slogan was canned; [Buzz] Aldrin's was spontaneous. He stepped down from the bottom rung of the ladder, looked around and uttered two words: "Magnificent desolation." It's not clear whether he was trying to be profound. One suspects not; some of the best lines come naturally. It's also doubtful that he realized the wider significance of what he was saying—the fact that he was providing the perfect two-word metaphor for the space program. As an achievement, the effort to land on the Moon was magnificent. It required the energy, enthusiasm, brilliance, and creativity, not to mention bravery, of thousands. But, as a process, it was desolate, devoid of meaning. All along, NASA publicists had worked hard to give that magnificently desolate endeavor ersatz [artificial] meaning. Their effort was crowned by Armstrong, who called it a giant leap for mankind. One of history's greatest ironies was that so much beauty and imagination was invested into a trip to a sterile rock of no purpose to anyone. Michael Collins, who orbited above the lunar explorers, recorded his reaction:

> The first thing that springs to mind is the vivid contrast between the Earth and the Moon. . . . I'm sure that to a geologist the Moon is a fascinating place, but this monotonous rock pile, this withered, Sun-seared peach pit out of my window offers absolutely no competition to the gem it orbits. Ah, the Earth, with its verdant valleys, its misty waterfalls. . . . I'd just like to get our job done and get out of here.

As James Irwin, the *Apollo 15* astronaut, once remarked, with more incisiveness than he realized, "Astronauts come back from the Moon, say it's great, but it has no atmosphere."

On the eve of *Apollo 11*'s launch, the veteran correspondent Eric Sevareid spoke of his feeling that the space adventure was nearing its denouement:

> We are a people who hate failure. It's un-American. It is a fair guess that the failure of *Apollo 11* would not curtail future space programs but re-energize them. Success may well curtail them because for a long time to come future flights will seem anti-climactic, chiefly of laboratory, not popular interest, and the pressure to divert these great sums of money to inner space, terra firma and inner man will steadily grow.

Norman Mailer, part of the press corps in Houston, noted how reporters didn't wait for Armstrong and Aldrin to finish their moon walk. They left the room en masse, without pausing to see what interesting rocks the astronauts might find. They had their story. The story was landing on the Moon. That's what all the effort and excitement, not to mention the sorrow and tragedy, of the previous ten years had all been about. The rest was just window dressing, an attempt to give a shallow challenge some scientific credibility. The reporters understood that the race was over.

NASA suggested as much when, shortly after the *Apollo 11* landing, they celebrated by flashing on the big screen at Mission Control Kennedy's famous words "Before this decade is out. . . . " Below was a simple message: "TASK ACCOMPLISHED, July 1969." The sense of conclusion was understandable, as was the triumphalism. But the message was nevertheless deeply symbolic of NASA's greatest difficulty, namely the desire of the agency to graft its grandiose dreams of limitless space exploration onto the much more prosaic and finite ambition of the American people to win a single race.

While Armstrong, Aldrin, and Collins were traveling to the Moon, Ralph Lapp, long a critic of the space program, remarked that scientists like him were looking forward to the landing so that NASA would be able to "wind up its manned space spectaculars and get on with the job of promoting space science." Apollo, he reminded his readers, will have cost taxpayers $25 billion. "Yet manned space flights will have given scientists very little information about space. Man, himself, has been the main experiment. And man is the principal reason why Project Apollo has cost so much money." His dream, he confessed, was that upon completion of the mission, Nixon would meet the astronauts and declare: "The people of the world salute your heroism. In the name of all the people on this planet . . . I declare the senseless space race ended. And now, gentlemen, let us point our science and technology in the direction of man."

The Apollo 11 Moon Landing Cannot Be Justified by Its Results

Hugo Young, Bryan Silcock, and Peter Dunn

In the following viewpoint, published soon after the Apollo 11 moon landing, British journalists argue that it increased American prestige only within the United States, and that its scientific and technological results could have been achieved at much lower cost through other means. Claims for its wider significance are, in their opinion, merely "mystical" rather than rational and cannot be substantiated in the foreseeable future. Hugo Young, Bryan Silcock, and Peter Dunn were journalists with the London *Times* and are authors of *Journey to Tranquility*, from which this viewpoint is taken.

SOURCE. Hugo Young, Bryan Silcock, and Peter Dunn, "Chapter 14: Meager Harvest," *Journey Toward Tranquility*. London, England: Jonathan Cape, 1969, pp. 292–296. Copyright © 1969. Reprinted by permission of The Random House Group Ltd. and The Times/NI Syndication nisyndication.com. All rights reserved.

There is, in fact only one part of the world where American prestige has incontrovertibly been lifted by Apollo, and that is in America itself. The moon landing was a source of fully justifiable pride to many Americans. It persuaded them, if not many other people, to believe more passionately in American capitalism and the American social system. Moreover, when it was begun, it was economically, politically and psychologically a convenient exercise for them to undertake.

Apollo may not have impinged greatly on American power in the world. Arguably, it is a rebuke to the immaturity of a nation which does not yet have the political will to remove the cancers which afflict it. But it has provided jobs for men and an outlet for ambitions which might otherwise have found far more harmful tasks to occupy them. In its own terms, it has been one unmistakable triumph to set beside the failures and miasmic confusions of the daily national grind at home and abroad. It may not have persuaded the world that America was a greater country than she was known to be already, but it has done something which should certainly not be discounted: in response to Sputnik and Gagarin, it stilled the demon of Americans' own belief in their inferiority.

That is a limited and inevitably transient achievement, very much smaller than Kennedy hoped for. America went to the moon to score a political triumph. She occupied Tranquility, but the triumph she sought eluded her. For this expensive blunder, therefore, some compensation must be discovered. Apollo did undeniably have results, even though they were not the results Americans were looking for in 1961. What exactly are these fortuitous by-products of Gagarin and the Bay of Pigs? Men did not go the moon in search of knowledge, but what knowledge have they come by?

The samples of the moon's crust which Armstrong and Aldrin brought back enabled geologists and astronomers to come closer to answering a problem on which speculation had fed for decades, if not centuries. Some of the samples showed unmistakable signs of having once been molten, a feature which virtually closed the debate about whether the moon was a hot or a cold body. Almost all schools of thought now agree that the moon was shaped both by volcanic activity and by meteoric impacts. Thus the argument has ended in stalemate: neither side was wholly right. Further samples retrieved by later Apollo missions will embellish this discovery. They may also help to resolve another pressing question, the question of the origin of the moon. Eventually there can be little doubt that the uncorrupted moon, "the Rosetta Stone of the solar system," will disclose infinitely more information about the history of the solar system than is obtainable on earth itself, even though the broader question of the nature of the universe is likely to remain little less murky than before.

> The cornucopia of knowledge which reposes in lifeless moon grit could quite feasibly, and much less expensively, have been opened by unmanned machines.

The rocks, of course, did not need man to bring them back. The cornucopia of knowledge which reposes in lifeless moon grit could quite feasibly, and much less expensively, have been opened by unmanned machines landing on the moon and being brought back by remote control. Now that men have done the job, that is a hypothetical point. But the distinction is profoundly relevant to the other scientific benefits of space.

Scientifically and practically the profits from the space program have been immense. The invention of the space satellite has produced advances many of which have barely begun to be exploited. In weather-forecasting, communications and navigation the bounty of space has already proved very lush. In charting the earth's resources—the location and movement of raw materials on and below the surface—the potential of space has still to

Sputnik, the first satellite in space, is shown next to a statue of Yuri Gagarin, the first man in space, at the Museum of Cosmonautics in Moscow. Although the Soviet Union was first in putting an artificial satellite and a man into orbit, the US moon landing ended the space race. (**Misha Japaridze/AP Images.**)

be put to its full practical use. In education, likewise, the uses of the satellite over large, unreachable populations in countries such as India offer measureless possibilities.

These, however, have nothing to do with Apollo. They are often cited as evidence of the value obtained from Apollo's billions. But it is false and ironic that they should be; for far from contributing to the new dimensions implicit in earth satellites, Apollo has if anything shrank them. Owing to the supreme urgency of Apollo, scientific and economic space projects were cut to the financial bone. It is significant that in the catalogues of "spin-off" which apologists for the space program grew accustomed to producing in order to persuade the American taxpayer that he was gaining some benefit from it, Apollo's fruits in the consumer economy were hard to find. They rarely went beyond such esoteric items as more protective fire-fighting suits and "filament-wound brassiere supports."

Clearly those are not the only technological by-products of the moon journey. Electronics, metallurgy, data processing, quality control procedures, instrumentation, medicine: these are all disciplines on which Apollo has made greater demands than ever before. Many parts of the economy were touched by space. Advances in a fantastically diverse area may be attributed to it. It is often hard to be sure how many of these sprang directly from Apollo, and not from other developments in space hardware. But the space program has indubitably been a "cutting edge" for American technology, and Apollo has been the cutting edge of the space program.

> "Will the intense excitement of the journey to Tranquility in July 1969 be more than a transient, empty, virtuoso performance?"

As justifications of Apollo, however, these are trivial offerings. They were strictly secondary consequences of the project. They do not explain why Apollo should have been undertaken in preference to some great project of earth-bound engineering, something with similar by-products but a more conspicuously beneficial focus. They are rationalizations after the event, and to many judges of mundane scientific priorities they sound sadly inadequate.

In the end, therefore, it would seem that Apollo is not to be judged by reason at all. It was done by reasoning men for thoroughly pragmatic motives, toward what they took to be a quick and visible result. But between what they sought and what they achieved there stands a very wide chasm. What they are left with is an exercise not in logic but in something close to mysticism: a ritual, supposedly lying deep among man's primitive aspirations, has been completed.

Had that proposition been spelled out before Apollo began, it might have been possible to discover whether

Sputnik and the Soviet Space Program

On October 4, 1957, the world was stunned by the news that the Soviet Union had put an artificial satellite named Sputnik into orbit. Such a thing had never been done before, and it made people nervous, because most knew nothing of space beyond what they had seen in science fiction movies about invasion from the sky. Furthermore, if the Soviets had the rocket power to launch satellites, it seemed likely that they could also launch missiles—although the first satellite itself was no larger than a basketball.

In addition to these fears, Americans were dismayed for another reason: it was a blow to discover that Soviet technology was ahead of US technology, something no one had suspected. There was a plan for developing a rocket called Vanguard to orbit a satellite for scientific purposes, but it had not been given high priority. In response to public demand, testing was rushed, and two months after Sputnik's launch Vanguard blew up on the pad while the world watched. The Space Race had begun.

During the next few years the Soviets achieved quite a few "firsts"— several unmanned moon probes, the first man in space, and the first space walk, among others—while the United

the aspiration to reach the moon is widespread among men and high among their unsatisfied desires, or whether it is the property of only a handful of dreamers. In fact this was not the proposition put to the world. Instead, it was obscured by argument that the journey to Tranquility would be *useful*—indeed, that it was imperative for the security of the nation which made it. Yet now that the journey is complete, the mysticism alone is left.

We are therefore invited to judge the completion of the ritual without serious reference to logic. Its value, the argument runs, is incapable of measurement against any rational criterion. Of course, attempts are made to rationalize it. The need to put man on the moon has been expounded in many intricate treatises on his special intelligence, his powers of observation, his ability to

States worked desperately to catch up, generally matching or exceeding Soviet feats quickly. The American effort to send men to the moon was a matter not just of Cold War strategy, but of regaining national pride.

Unlike the United States, the Soviet Union kept its space program secret and did not disclose its many failures. NASA had to assume that the next Soviet achievement might occur at any moment, and a number of missions, notably Apollo 8, were moved ahead on the basis of suspected Russian plans. The Soviets strove to be first on the moon until shortly before US astronauts landed there. But after the moon landing, to save face, the Soviets claimed that they had never aimed for a manned lunar mission. This assertion was accepted by the American media, and as a result books written in the 1970s and 1980s sometimes argue that the Apollo program had been unnecessary. Not until twenty years later, when the Cold War was ending, did the Soviet government admit that they had indeed tried to develop the capability to send humans to the moon. Detailed information about their moon program was not declassified until after the Soviet Union's collapse.

select the information he wishes to retrieve, the contributions he can make to science. But these are disguises for a romantic and irrational leap. We are told that man must go. But no impressive body of questions which the exploit is intended to answer has ever been formulated. As one sceptical scientist, Dr. Philip Abelson, has said, "Nowhere in the program for manned exploration of the moon and planets is there a hint of major future development of a puzzling body of facts or even speculations that could fall into place as a major new enlightenment."

As the pragmatic case for the moon visibly dwindled, the mystical argument grew more pervasive. And, despite its unscientific quality, scientists themselves have been found among its most compassionate exponents. Harold Urey, one of America's foremost physicists, epitomized it when he compared Apollo with the building of great monuments. "The real reason for undertaking the space program," he once said, "is an innate characteristic of human beings, namely, some curious drive to try to do what might be thought to be impossible—to try to excel in one way or another. . . . These drives of people are akin to other activities such as building the Parthenon and the temples of the ancient world, the building of St. Peter's with its marvelous decorations at a time when it represented real sacrifice on the part of people. . . . The space program in a way is our cathedral which we are building."

The great question which this analogy begs is how enduring the cathedral of the moon will be. St. Peter's and the Parthenon still stand. They can be appreciated as intensely today as they were when they were erected. The sacrifice left a life-enhancing residue. Will the landing on the moon leave a similar mark? Will the intense excitement of the journey to Tranquility in July 1969 be more than a transient, empty, virtuoso performance?

Very large claims have been made for its significance. Hugh Dryden, when he was second in command at NASA, claimed, "The impact can only be compared with those great developments of past history, like the Copernican theory which placed the sun, rather than the earth, at the center of our solar system; the work of Sir Isaac Newton in relating the fall of an apple to the notion of the moon round the earth through the universal law of gravitation; to the industrial revolution." A comparison more insistently made is between men landing on the moon and the first fish which flopped on to land and struggled to become an amphibian.

All that can be said of this is that it will take decades, very possibly centuries, to substantiate. The omens, so far as they can now be perceived, are not very encouraging. The moon is totally hostile to man. It offers no possibility of easy habitation or economic exploitation.

Nor is there yet any compelling reason why men should seek to convert it into a retreat and an escape from earth, as an alternative to solving the problems of the world. Conceivably, such a reason may one day emerge. Conceivably, the capacity to populate the moon will one day be relevant to

> "The moon is totally hostile to man. It offers no possibility of easy habitation or economic exploitation."

man. Conceivably, the scientific residue of Apollo will be found in problems which no one has even asked. But we should not be cowed by the immensity of Apollo's triumph into ignoring the rational probability that no such product will soon be seen.

This is the truth which must be faced in any consideration of man's future role on the moon or other planets. A decision to go further cannot be convincingly represented as a bid for immediate world prestige or identifiable scientific discovery. Apollo has shown that those objectives, although they may be made to attract the support of the mass of men for the enterprise, are in fact chimerical. In sending men to Mars, it will be the act itself which counts, the great instinctual leap.

When he wound up the proceedings of Apollo 11, George Mueller pleaded for man to continue and expand his adventures in space or else "fall back from his destiny." "The mighty surge of his achievement will be lost," Mueller went on, . . . "and the confines of this planet will destroy it." This, although it comes from a scientist, is not a statement of fact or even of reasonable speculation.

It is a godlike prophecy, from a man with no greater claim to an accurate vision of the future than other men. It is, however, with its intimations of problems unknown and uncontemplated, the only impulse which will propel men further than the moon. Unadorned by reason or logic, it is the proposition which men must examine as they attempt to determine whether journeys beyond

Tranquility are a necessary gratification of their primitive instincts, or an insane distraction from the real work of the world.

The Apollo 11 Moon Landing Was Not a Waste of Money

Globe and Mail

The following editorial was published in Canada's national news-paper, the *Globe and Mail*, on the day after the Apollo 11 moon landing. The newspaper does not agree with those who call the moon landing a waste of resources and money. It expresses the editors' belief that it was the first step toward future travel to other planets, which was important because eventually Earth will be destroyed by changes in the sun. In the past, most great technological advances were made under the pressure of war, but the moon landing—to its credit, according to the writers— was achieved in peacetime. In their opinion, not only would the moon landing provide great benefits to Earth, but it had shown what humans can achieve if they choose to pursue a goal.

Man took the first step yesterday from earth to infinity. When Neil Armstrong and Edwin Aldrin brought their Eagle to a stop on the moon, they proved that human beings can leave this planet for another, and beyond that another and another, until perhaps—probably—they can slip out of their own solar system, their own universe. All the stars are on the travel maps for their descendants. They are no longer earthbound. Eternity can be theirs.

This planet earth will die. Five billion years from now its life will have been lived. But from what distant spheres will its children watch that final burst of flame and finish? The power to do it now is theirs.

Only in momentary, rather painful stretches of the mind can one comprehend the possibilities that reach down the light years of time. But they are concrete, practical. Whatever the end of this first great adventure, there will be others. Men will land on the moon again, and after the moon on Mars. At first they will establish only temporary way stations, and then—it is not today too much to believe—there could be colonies. Some children of the future may see the sun for the first time from another planet. Some may see a different sun. Always beyond each landing will be a new world, a new universe.

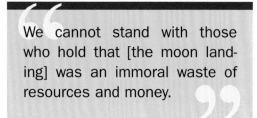

> We cannot stand with those who hold that [the moon landing] was an immoral waste of resources and money.

If we doubt it the matter-of-factness of the men on the moon says it is so, and the quips of Michael Collins as he orbits in Columbia awaiting their return give it all a human dimension. Everest was there, so they climbed it. The heavens are there. . . .

A Sound Investment

This mission which began eight years and ten months ago, when President John F. Kennedy set United States'

sights on the moon, will undoubtedly go into history as the greatest achievement of the Kennedy and [Lyndon B.] Johnson administration. It has been criticized. We cannot stand with those who hold that it was an immoral waste of resources and money. Even on a pure, hard-line basis of value almost instantly received it will probably stand up as a sound investment.

In humanity's past, most of the great inventive and productive periods have been periods of war when a nation's whole resources became available to achieve the single objective—survival. Looking no further back than the Second World War, it becomes impossible to count the benefits that single period of concentration produced for human beings.

This is the first time a program of such gargantuan proportions has been launched and carried through in peace time. One that said nothing was too expen-

Distant Earthlike planets—such as the one discovered by Swiss scientists in 2007 and shown in an artist's rendition—might one day be home to spacefaring humans. (Salvatore Di Nolfi/AP Images.)

> The price paid to enable Apollo XI to wrench our eyes from terrestrial suburbs to the real estate in the skies is very practically no more than a down payment on a better life on earth.

sive, nothing too impossible to try. One that brought together such vast amounts of incentive energy, that combined so many scientists of so many different disciplines to adapt and change and devised new processes. All without the dreadful price of war.

The fallout of benefits for men on earth—let alone those who journey outward—cannot be computed save by those very computers that have come so swiftly to their present sophistication largely because of this program. The price paid to enable Apollo XI to wrench our eyes from terrestrial suburbs to the real estate in the skies is very practically no more than a down payment on a better life on earth. The hardware it produces to make industry more efficient, recreation more enjoyable, problems more solvable is alone worth this initial cost.

Proof of What Humans Can Accomplish

But beyond all that it has taught us what men can do if they will. It has given us a system by which we can lick the problems of earth if we choose to lick them. If we select our objectives and put behind them the same concentration of money, resources, energy, inventiveness and enthusiasm, there is nothing we cannot accomplish, whether it is feeding the hungry, cleansing our earthly environment or mending the differences between races and nations.

Indeed, it is possible that Apollo and its comparable Soviet Union program may lead us to co-operative space programs that will thaw the cold war here on earth. Despite our divisions it is possible to be pleased that Luna [a Soviet spacecraft] was breathing down the U.S. astronauts' necks.

It was also possible to be pleased that at the moment of landing it took a man to save the machine. Eagle by itself might have ploughed into those rocks that Neil Armstrong lifted it over.

Men and their machines. They have done it. And now, if they can refrain long enough from blowing up their launching pad, the moon can be their stepping stone to the stars.

Enthusiasm for the Apollo Moon Landings Did Not Last

Monika Gisler and Didier Sornette

In the following viewpoint, Swiss scholars describe the enthusiastic response to the Apollo 11 moon landing and point out that it did not last. By the time of the second moon landing the public had become apathetic and the voices of critics had grown stronger. In intellectual and political circles it became fashionable to ridicule the project, they say, while NASA increasingly focused on technical and scientific goals that did not inspire non-scientists and were seen by many as incompatible with social welfare. President Richard Nixon was not interested in continuing the Apollo program, and so it was terminated in 1972. However, the authors argue, it was an example of the kind of event that sometimes occurs in history, in which over-enthusiasm and risk-taking lead to innovation that would not otherwise occur. Didier Sornette is a professor and director of the Financial Crisis Observatory at the Swiss Federal Institute of

Technology in Zurich, Switzerland. Monika Gisler was a research fellow there at the time this paper was written.

The Apollo program provides a vivid illustration of a societal bubble, defined as a collective over-enthusiasm as well as unreasonable investments and efforts, derived through excessive public and/or political expectations of positive outcomes associated with a general reduction of risk aversion. . . .

We contend that bubbles seem to be an unavoidable development in technological and social enterprise that benefits society by allowing exceptional niches of innovation to be explored. During bubbles, people take inordinate risks that would not otherwise be justified by standard cost-benefit and portfolio analysis. Bubbles are characterized by collective over-enthusiasm as well as unreasonable investments and efforts, derived through excessive public and/or political expectations of positive outcomes. Only during these times do people dare explore new opportunities, many of them unreasonable and hopeless, with rare emergences of lucky achievements. [Didier] Sornette proposed this mechanism as the leading one controlling the appearance of disruptive innovations and major advances. Bubbles, defined as collective over-enthusiasm, seem a necessary (and unavoidable) evil to foster our collective attitude towards risk taking and break the stalemate of society resulting from its tendency towards stronger risk avoidance. An absence of bubble psychology would lead to stagnation and conservatism as no large risks are taken and, as a consequence, no large return can be accrued. . . .

Building Apollo was more than just the yearning to beat the Russians. It was the fulfillment of a dream, be it a boy's dream, a dream fueled by the heaps of science fiction narratives or even the vision to build a better society in space. And it did not free the impassionate

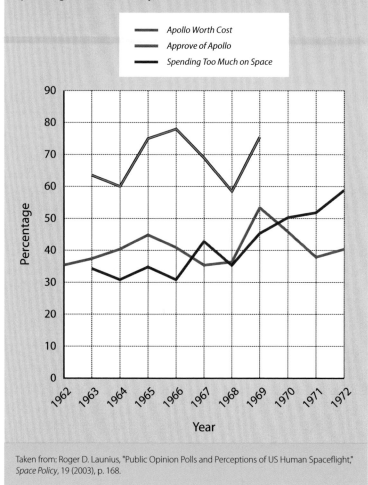

PUBLIC SUPPORT FOR THE APOLLO PROGRAM

Despite the widespread enthusiasm for the Apollo 11 moon landing at the time it occurred, fewer people approved of the effort to reach the moon than were excited by it, and most of the time fewer than 50 percent of the public was in favor of spending as much money as it cost.

Apollo Worth Cost
Approve of Apollo
Spending Too Much on Space

Percentage

Year

Taken from: Roger D. Launius, "Public Opinion Polls and Perceptions of US Human Spaceflight," *Space Policy*, 19 (2003), p. 168.

participants until the dream of the lunar landing was fulfilled. As *Los Angeles Times* reporter Rudy Abramson has put it in 1969—just three days before the *Apollo 11* launch—"The United States this week will commit its national pride, eight years of work and $24 billion of its fortune to showing the world it can still fulfill a dream." After all, taking risks was not seen as putting one's life in danger, but [as] getting the chance to explore things, to experience space exploration. . . .

The Public Response

Launches from Cape Canaveral inevitably drew hundreds of thousands of excited spectators; public support of the space program in its early stage was enthusiastic. It was the time when Congress decided that NASA, and not NASA *and* the Air Force, would put a man on the Moon. During the negotiations, John Glenn and Scott Carpenter had orbited the Earth, and the American public was cheering for its new space agency. In 1962, the high volume of sales of space toys and kits in department stores after each launch was proof of the public attraction to anything related to space. As early as 1963, however, criticism was beginning to grow in the press. Whereas in 1962, the editors used superlatives when talking of space exploration, in 1963, enthusiasm was somewhat low. The lavish amount of money being poured into NASA was being questioned, should it go up constantly. A number of writers criticized the program as a cynical mix of public relations and profit-seeking, a massive drain of tax funds away from serious domestic ills of the decade, a technological high card in international tensions during the cold war era. The last orbital flight had been in May 1963 and it looked very ordinary compared to the Soviet double act. A series of congressional hearing questioned the value of a lunar program. Among scientists, the initial enchantment had faded before the mounting costs and they feared the heavy drain on other fields of scientific endeavor. Furthermore, less and less was heard of the military urgency of exploring the Moon; even the Air Force decided its interests would lie more in "inner-space" capability. Payoffs of the program seemed to vanish. As a consequence, in July 1963, the *New York Times* carried a headline proclaiming *Lunar Program In Crisis*, echoing popular sentiments. What has happened? The impetus for this declaration was not only managerial problems within NASA but foremost a study concluding that the odds of reaching the Moon by the end of the decade were only about one in ten and that a lunar landing could not be attempted "with acceptable risk" until late 1971. Others criticized the Apollo program for its timetable, for being developed in the context of a race rather than as an undertaking following a reasonable pace. . . .

All the same, the pendulum again swung towards the space program. After this temporary drop of enthusiasm in 1963, polls in the spring and fall of 1964 showed 64–69 percent of the public were favorably disposed to landing an American on the Moon, with 78 percent saying the Apollo program should be maintained at its current pace or speed up. Arguments on both economic and technological levels paid their tributes.

> [Apollo] created a general new awareness of the Earth, as representing 'a grand oasis in the big vastness of space.'

Polls performed in summer 1965 showed a new decrease to a certain extent, since a third of the nation now favored cutting the space budget, while only 16 percent wanted to increase it. Over the next three and a half years, support for cutting space spending went up to 40 percent, with those preferring an increase dropping to 14 percent. At the end of 1967, the *New York Times* reported that a poll conducted in six American cities showed that five other public issues held priority over efforts on outer space. . . .

The efforts of 1966–67, however, paid their tributes: On Christmas morning of 1968, the Americans were greeted by newspapers, radio and television reports with the momentous news that the crew of *Apollo 8* was on its way back to Earth after becoming the first human beings to orbit the Moon. For the United States space program, this endeavor represented a major step toward achieving the national goal, and gaining support with it. The news that three astronauts had flown around the Moon sparked feelings of national pride. This event stood in stark contrast to the previous events of 1968 (the Vietnam war still going on, the assassinations of M.L. King and R. Kennedy, among others). The nation was becoming increasingly divided over the issues escalating during this year. *Apollo 8* provided an uplifting end to all these negative events. One of the telegrams the astronauts received from the public summarizes well the general spirit associated with *Apollo 8* mission: "You [i.e. the astronauts] saved 1968."

In particular, this event created a general new awareness of the Earth, as representing "a grand oasis in the big vastness of space," as astronaut [James] Lovell expressed it, overheard by millions of people during a television broadcast by the astronauts from lunar orbit. This made *Apollo 8* different from previous explorations. Many observers have noted the coincidence between *Apollo 8* and increase in environmental activism.

The historical impact of *Apollo 8* was only equaled when *Apollo 11* made it to the Moon on July 19, 1969. An estimated 600 million people—one fifth of the world's population—witnessed it on television and radio. Some observers designated the day as a turning point in history. Scientific writer Robert Heinlein, who had penned the story for the 1950 film *Destination Moon*, named it the "[. . .] greatest event in all the history of the human race up to this time."

After *Apollo 11* had landed on the Moon, lunar scientists as well as astronauts became highly optimistic about the outcome of scientific research associated with orbiting flights and exploration of the Moon. Astronauts had demonstrated that men were able to function as explorers in the lunar environment (Michael Collins, as an example). They were viewed by the advocates for manned space flight as ample justification for the enormous investment they required. Hopes of the scientists for resolving major questions about the origin and evolution of the Moon reached a peak of optimism at the beginning of 1970.

> " NASA tended to emphasize the technical elements of the program rather than the human experiences that would have been easier to understand. "

The Aftermath

The international chariot race, however, ended when the Eagle landed. With astonishing rapidity, the raison d'être [reason for being] of the Apollo program had undergone a metamorphosis. Overnight, it transformed into a scientific undertaking for the highest intellectual purpose. By the spring of 1970, it was obvious that the intellectual rationale for Apollo could not justify the full program in the absence of enthusiastic public support, and that was waning. In November 1969, *Apollo 12* astronauts achieved a second lunar landing and made two Moonwalks. Once again, there were live pictures, but the news coverage was showing signs of apathy. One Tennessee resident was even quoted as naming the event an "old hat." The second landing on the Moon lacked of enthusiasm, the public progressively more disenchanted with the space program. The voice of Apollo's critics—always there but never very loud—thus began to swell in volume. It became an amusement to ridicule the program in intellectual and political circles; support began to wither. The national polls in the summer of 1969 found that 53 percent of the country was opposed to a manned mission to Mars. And a poll taken in 1973 showed that only foreign aid had less support than space exploration. Failures of the *Apollo 13* mission added fuel to the fires of criticisms. Also within NASA, the administrators sensed that subsequent missions could not afford any other failure.

There were several factors that exacerbated the decline in interest. . . . NASA tended to emphasize the technical elements of the program rather than the human experiences that would have been easier to understand. Lunar science became increasingly the focus of astronauts as well as mission planners. For nonscientists, geologic talk about the Moon and the origin of Earth wasn't easy to follow. The cultural divide between scientists and the rest seemed to grow. From a practical standpoint, only a handful of Earth scientists was benefiting from Apollo to pursue research of questionable social relevance at enormous expense, to the deprivation not only of more immediate and pressing social needs, but also of other "relevant" scientific goals. This attitude spread through many sectors of American society that had supported space research enthusiastically a few years earlier, notably academia. Liberals equated the funding of technological development and fundamental scientific inquiry (except in the field of medical research) as being indifferent to social welfare. The same attitude was adopted by the military establishment and its committees in Congress. . . .

In the short term, Project Apollo was an American triumph. In the long term, the costs, close to 25 billion USD overall in 1960s dollars, were large and might have made a difference in other programs or helped avoid the inflation that fueled dissatisfaction during the Vietnam War. Furthermore, we now know that the reason for the Soviet Union loss of the cold war was that it could not compete with Western financial and corporate power. From the beginning, the Soviets were behind in almost every kind of technologically complicated armament. Actually, the Soviet Union took its position in space out of weakness. It developed its space program based on less advanced technology (but more robust as shown by the exceptional robustness of its MIR space stations and the use of its old technology launchers by the United States

Despite his warm, public welcome to the returning Apollo 11 crew, President Richard Nixon (right) ended the Apollo program in 1972. (**AP Images.**)

and many other nations after the end of the cold war). On the American side, the lack of transparency of the USSR produced a series of efforts to find out what the Soviets, were doing. The Sputnik I launch led directly to that of the first reconnaissance satellite by the United States early in 1961, and in turn inspired the Soviets to other space endeavors. The moves and countermoves did not all fit together neatly, but the Soviet accomplishments brought the Americans into a full-scale, open race for the Moon. Although the Moon program contributed a great deal to the United States, one could argue that the tens of billions of dollars spent in the 1960s on what [President John F.] Kennedy essentially thought of as world propaganda could have been otherwise devoted to the United States' domestic economy or even defense, and that might have convinced the Soviets more quickly of the fruitlessness of the tragic conflict with the United States.

> The enthusiasm did not out-live by much the first Moon landing, and a general positive sentiment in favor of the Moon exploration started to fade shortly after the first step on the Moon.

A Unique Event

Today, more than three decades after the program ended, Apollo remains a unique event in the history of space exploration. It was one of the most exceptional and costly projects ever undertaken by the United States, and thus constitutes an excellent example of how bubbles function from within. In the context of bubbles associated with innovation ventures and the creation of new technology, the Apollo Project demonstrated the large risks that have been undertaken individually, politically and financially, leading to a collective (individual, public and political) over-enthusiasm, which played a very significant role in the development and completion of the process as such. The qualifier "over" emphasizes that the enthusiasm did not out-live by much the first Moon landing, and a general positive sentiment in favor of the Moon exploration started to fade shortly after the first step on the Moon. The evidence gathered here supports the view that the Apollo program was a genuine bubble, . . . with little long-term fundamental support either from society or from a technical or scientific viewpoint. As expected from our hypothesis on bubbles, it led to innumerable technological innovations, and scientific advances, but many of them at a cost documented to be disproportionate compared with the returns. These returns may turn out to be positive in the long run as many of its fruits remain to be fully appreciated and exploited.

With the first landing on the Moon in 1969, it was the general belief at the time that thirty years later at the transition to the third millennium, mankind would have established permanent stations on the Moon and on Mars, with space travel expected to become almost routine and open to commercial exploitation for the public. With the hindsight of 2008, it is easy to dismiss this view. Here, we stress instead that this view exemplifies the bubble spirit which is typical rather than exceptional. Enthusiasm was always present to push for the endeavor, risk always a topic but never an issue. Major risks have been accepted by individuals, first of all by some of the pioneers (engineers, astronauts). They did not shy away from taking all possible types of risks, even at the costs of their own life or health. Such high risk levels were accepted for "real reasons," in the sense summarized by today's NASA administrator Michael Griffin in January 2007. Real reasons are intuitive and compelling, but they are not logical, they are not the standard acceptable logical reasons based on solid rational cost/benefit analysis. Real reasons are the opposite; they include curiosity, quest for the fulfillment of dreams, competitiveness (because people want to leave a legacy), and challenge, for the sheer reason that it's there. Even during Apollo's last years, the launch team's esprit de corps seemed to be of central concern. It could in fact be seen as a personal commitment of each member of the launch team.

Enthusiasm shown by the public and by the financially responsible entity, the Congress, was on the other hand somewhat more complex. Commitment by the

> Just as Apollo had come out of nowhere, and held center stage for a decade, it vanished from the public consciousness, as if it had never happened.

public was swaying. It did not always stand with NASA in equal measure, thus was not always agreeing on taking the risks that went with investing in such a major endeavor. . . .

Since [President Richard] Nixon was not interested in pursuing the "Apollo idea," it terminated in 1972. This ending though did not come as surprising as it seemed at first sight, since its decline loomed on the horizon some years before, after 1965 from the public's, after 1967 from Congress' side.

We have called the Apollo program one of the most exceptional and costly projects ever undertaken by the United States at peacetime. However, just as Apollo had come out of nowhere, and held center stage for a decade, it vanished from the public consciousness, as if it had never happened. It thus was an exceptional niche, not having been revisited to any significant degree ever since.

The Apollo Moon Missions Started the Environmental Movement

Robert Poole

In the following viewpoint, a British historian describes how the sight of Earth from the moon had an unexpected effect on the public: It made people aware of the need to preserve Earth's environment. Before the trips to the moon, no ship had been far enough away from Earth to see it whole, as a globe, and no one really knew what it would look like. Everyone was struck by its beauty, and many developed environmental awareness, which before long was transforming American culture. Some people lost interest in humankind's future in space entirely, even though without the moon program, the importance of protecting the home planet might never have been recognized.

SOURCE. Robert Poole, "Chapter 1: Earthrise, seen for the first time by human eyes," *Earthrise: How Man First Saw the Earth*. New Haven: Yale University Press, 2010. Copyright © 2010 by Yale University Press. All rights reserved. Reproduced by permission.

Robert Poole teaches at the University of Cumbria in Lancaster, England.

On Christmas Eve 1968 three American astronauts were in orbit around the Moon: Frank Borman, James Lovell and Bill Anders. The crew of Apollo 8 had been declared by the United Nations to be the "envoys of mankind in outer space"; they were also its eyes. They were already the first people to leave Earth's orbit, the first to set eyes on the whole Earth, and the first to see the dark side of the Moon, but the most powerful experience still awaited them. For three orbits they gazed down on the lunar surface through their capsule's tiny windows as they carried out the checks and observations prescribed for almost every minute of this tightly planned mission.

On the fourth orbit, as they began to emerge from the far side of the Moon, something happened. They were still out of radio contact with the Earth, but the onboard voice recorder captured their excitement.

Borman: Oh my God! Look at that picture over there! Here's the Earth coming up. Wow, that is pretty!

Anders: Hey, don't take that, it's not scheduled.

Borman: (Laughter). You got a colour film, Jim?

Anders: Hand me that roll of colour quick, will you—

Lovell: Oh man, that's great!

Anders: Hurry. Quick . . .

Lovell: Take several of them! Here, give it to me . . .

Borman: Calm down, Lovell.

The crew of Apollo had seen the Earth rise. The commander, Frank Borman, later recalled the moment.

I happened to glance out of one of the still-clear windows just at the moment the Earth appeared over the lunar horizon. It was the most beautiful, heart-catching sight of my life, one that sent a torrent of nostalgia, of sheer homesickness, surging through me. It was the only thing in space that had any color to it. Everything else was either black or white, but not the Earth.

"Raging nationalistic interests, famines, wars, pestilences don't show from that distance," he commented afterwards. "We are one hunk of ground, water, air, clouds, floating around in space. From out there it really is 'one world.'" "Up there, it's a black-and-white world," explained James Lovell. "There's no color. In the whole universe, wherever we looked, the only bit of color was back on Earth. . . . It was the most beautiful thing there was to see in all the heavens. People down here don't realize what they have." Bill Anders recalled how the moment of Earthrise "caught us hardened test pilots."

We'd spent all our time on Earth training about how to study the Moon, how to go to the Moon; it was very lunar orientated. And yet when I looked up and saw the Earth coming up on this very stark, beat up lunar horizon, an Earth that was the only color that we could see, a very fragile looking Earth, a very delicate looking Earth, I was immediately almost overcome by the thought that here we came all this way to the Moon, and yet the most significant thing we're seeing is our own home planet, the Earth.

An Unexpected Focus on Earth

Looking back after twenty years, Anders told a reporter that although he now thought only occasionally about those events, "it was that Earth that really stuck in my mind when I think of Apollo 8. It was a surprise; we didn't think about that."

Like the crew of Apollo 8, NASA was so preoccupied with the Moon that it too forgot about the Earth. Photographs of Earth hardly featured at all on the official mission plans; they belonged in a miscellaneous category labelled "targets of opportunity" and given the lowest priority. As for the television camera that would provide the first live pictures of the Earth, the coverage was amateurish and ill-prepared: there was trouble with the telephoto lenses, the camera was hard to aim and the capsule windows were fogged. . . .

> " The sight of Earth came with the force of a revelation, a sense which deepened as the excitement of Apollo faded. "

This general lack of preparedness had one important effect on all concerned: the sight of Earth came with the force of a revelation, a sense which deepened as the excitement of Apollo faded. After watching the last Apollo launch, the New Age philosopher William Irwin Thompson wrote: "the recovery of our lost cosmic orientation will probably prove to be more historically significant than the design of the Saturn V rocket." The writer Norman Cousins told the 1975 Congressional hearings on the future of the space programme: "what was most significant about the lunar voyage was not that men set foot on the Moon, but that they set eye on the Earth."

This was not what had been supposed to happen. The cutting edge of the future was to be in space; Earth was the launchpad, not the target. . . .

Everywhere, newspaper editors wrote about the brotherhood of man and the spiritual unity of mankind.

The weekly magazines had the advantage of being able to print the newly released photographs of Earth. *Time* advertised its end-of-year number with a photograph of Earthrise and the single word, "Dawn." *Life*, in a New Year issue read (it was claimed) by one in four Americans, presented a sumptuous photo-essay on the mission, with the Earth filling a cover bearing the

To Preserve Earth's Biosphere, Humanity Must Use Resources from Space

Long before the lunar program had been carried to its successful conclusion, the budget began to decline. . . . Instead of a beginning, Apollo became an end. A crisis of the spirit had taken hold.

Ironically, the pictures of Earth taken from great distance by the Apollo astronauts contributed to this change. The view of our planet as a shimmering blue gem on the black velvet of space generated not only a more enlightened and knowledgeable perspective of the terrestrial environment, coupled with thoughtful concern regarding our environment and mankind's course,

it also conjured in many minds the less enlightened neo-Ptolemaic [Earth-centered] specter of a closed world in the center of so-called hostile nothingness, surrounded by dead, and so-called useless, worlds. . . .

As mankind, we have to pay a price for preserving our living standards, assuring a more humane quality of life in the less privileged countries, where the industrial revolution must still be completed, and preserving our biosphere. Rejecting the extraterrestrial option will, at best, be profoundly distressing.

The ultimate heritage of Apollo,

headline: "The Incredible Year '68." Inside was a poster-sized double-page spread of the Earthrise photo, and lines from the poet James Dickey: "Behold / The blue planet steeped in its dream / Of reality."

One commentary stood out above all others: the poet Archibald MacLeish's essay "Riders on the Earth." "For the first time in all of time," he wrote, "men have seen the Earth: seen it not as continents or oceans from the little distance of a hundred miles or two or three, but seen it from the depths of space; seen it whole and round and beautiful and small." This view, he prophesied, would remake mankind's image of itself. "To see the Earth as it truly is, small and blue and beautiful in that eternal silence where it floats, is to see ourselves as riders on the Earth together, brothers on that bright loveliness therefore, is a world that today is no more closed than it is flat. Soon we will no longer be limited to the biosphere as our all-supplying womb. We have been delivered into a larger world that is open to the universe. . . . Until now we were allowed to prey on the biosphere, on fossils and other conveniently placed resources. Now we are asked to show that we can do more than exploit already-made abundance—that we can create abundance from inexhaustible primordial sources. . . .

Earth is not an isolated space ship, but travels in the convoy of our star— a luxurious passenger liner, floating through galactic space along with a

giant power station and many freighters. Let us not tear up the stateroom furniture to use it for resources. We can board the freighters. It was done on July 20, 1969! The human dimension of Apollo's heritage is a message of hope and confidence, of growth and fulfillment of the human potential—in brief, of a greater and potentially better world, if we make it so. Then, Apollo will have been a beginning after all.

SOURCE. *Krafft A. Ehricke, "The Heritage of Apollo,"* Krafft Ehricke's Extraterrestrial Imperative, *ed. Marsha Freeman. Apogee Books, 2008.*

in the eternal cold—brothers who know that they are truly brothers." MacLeish's words [were] featured in the *New York Times* on Christmas Day, as the TV pictures of Earth and the Genesis broadcast still resonated in the mind. They were widely quoted again a few days later when the Earthrise photo appeared, and were extensively syndicated across the American and British press. It was the single most widely admired evocation of the spirit of Apollo 8.

The Beginning of Environmental Awareness

A newer strand of thought rose with the Earth: reverence for the environment. "No man ever before has looked at the world in one piece and told us about it," said the

> Looking back, it is possible to see that Earthrise marked the tipping point, the moment when the sense of the space age flipped from what it meant for space to what it meant for the Earth.

Sunday Denver Post. "Perhaps with the new understanding will come reverence for our planetary home and for the uniqueness of life." "We should cherish our home planet," advised the *Christian Science Monitor.* "Men must conserve the Earth's resources. They must protect their planetary environment from spreading pollution. They have no other sanctuary in the solar system. This, perhaps, is the most pertinent message for all of us that the astronauts bring back from the Moon." Looking back, it is possible to see that Earthrise marked the tipping point, the moment when the sense of the space age flipped from what it meant for space to what it meant for the Earth.

A few far-sighted thinkers noticed this rising Earth-awareness quite early on. [English physicist] C.P. Snow suggested that Apollo, "as well as being the greatest exploration . . . was very near the final one," and prophesied that civilisation would be "driven inward" by it. "How drab and grey, unappealing and insignificant, this planet would be without the radiance of life," wrote the microbiologist René Dubos. "I think the greatest contribution of Apollo has been to convert all those abstract ideas, like Spaceship Earth and global ecology, into an awareness that there is something unique about Earth and therefore something unique about man." The biophysicist John Platt wrote: "the great picture of Earth taken from the Moon is one of the most powerful images in the minds of men today and may be worth the cost of the whole Apollo project. It is changing our relationship to the Earth and to each other. I see that as a great landmark in exploration—to get away from the Earth to see it whole."

Fifteen months later, the US was celebrating the first Earth Day. Just beforehand, a correspondent to the magazine *Science*, John Caffrey, wrote: "I date my own reawakening of interest in man's environment to the Apollo 8 mission and to the first clear photographs of Earth from that mission . . . I suspect that the greatest lasting benefit of the Apollo missions may be, if my hunch is correct, this sudden rush of inspiration to try to save this fragile environment—the whole one—if we still can." Almost exactly four years after Apollo 8, the last of the Apollo missions brought back a still more famous photograph, the "Blue marble" shot of the full Earth. It was, wrote the ecologist Donald Worster, "a stunning revelation. . . . Its thin film of life . . . was far thinner and far more vulnerable than anyone had ever imagined." Suddenly the image of the Earth was everywhere; it seemed to some to mark "a new phase of civilisation," the beginning of the "age of ecology." It has been called "the most influential environmental photograph ever taken."

> Suddenly the image of the Earth was everywhere; it seemed to some to mark 'a new phase of civilisation,' the beginning of the 'age of ecology.'

Since then, the phrase "blue planet" has come to be bound up with the idea of caring for the Earth. It has been used as the name of a long-running children's series on American public TV with an environmental theme, of a stunning British nature documentary series on the life of the oceans, and of a NASA programme to map every square kilometre of the Earth's environment from space, to name but three. Yet until the mid-1960s, no one really knew what colour the Earth would be. Imaginative pictures of the Earth from space, such as Chesley Bonestell's 1952 space station, show something rather like the traditional blue and green geographical globe, the land (usually north America) prominent and clearly defined, the oceans greenish, and the clouds optimistically few. When the whole Earth was finally photographed clearly there was surprise at the dominance of dazzling blue ocean,

Apollo 8's view of the Earth as a patch of color amid a field of black and white in all directions galvanized environmental attitudes. (AP Images.)

the jacket of cloud and the relative invisibility of the land and of human settlement. The sight of Earth seemed humbling, a rebuke to the vanity of humankind—just as ancient philosophers had foreseen.

The Result of the View from Space

The idea that environmental awareness has in some way been bound up with the sight of the Earth from space has been often proposed but rarely investigated; few people, and still fewer historians, are interested in both the environment and the space programme. Yet, as [space journalist] Andrew Smith has observed, "there seem to have been two sharply delineated space programmes running parallel within the programme—an official one about engineering and flying and beating the Soviets, and an unofficial, almost clandestine other about people and their place in the universe; about consciousness, God, mind, life." It is this unofficial space programme that interests us now. Two remarkable films have brought home to a later generation the sheer magic of the first space age: Al Reinert's *For All Mankind*, and David Sington's *In the Shadow of the Moon*. Both focus on the experiences of the astronauts and both linger on the view of Earth from space.

> The biggest cultural change of all associated with the view of the whole Earth [was] the rise of environmentalism.

That view was presented afresh to public attention in Michael Light's exhibition *Full Moon*. Put together for the thirtieth anniversary of the Moon landings, it displayed magnificently restored copies of some of the Apollo photographs, including room-sized panoramas of the lunar landscape. What prompted most comment among reviewers was that even in colour, the Moon was still black and white. One photograph was not enlarged. In a doorway between two parts of the exhibition was a small blob of colour floating over a bone-dead landscape. The caption was if anything more arresting than the picture: "Earthrise, seen for the first time by human eyes." "Earthrise" alone was striking enough; "seen for the first time" introduced a historical perspective; but why add "by human eyes"? What other eyes might have seen this view, and how long ago? The perspective expanded again, to embrace all life in the universe, and all time since the Creation. . . .

The biggest cultural change of all associated with the view of the whole Earth [was] the rise of environmentalism. An "eco-renaissance" took place during the Apollo years of 1968–72, framed almost exactly by the "Earthrise" and "Blue marble" photographs four years apart. These were the years of the legendary *Whole Earth Catalog*, Friends of the Earth, and Earth Day, with environmentalism flowing into the anti-nuclear weapons crusade of the 1980s which also took the whole Earth as its emblem. These movements turned against the space programme, but they owed much of their early inspiration to its most important product: the image of the Earth. . . .

The idea that the Earth is alive owed both its inspiration and its influence to the sight of Earth from space. This kind of holistic thinking about the Earth took root during the first space age and has been spreading gradually ever since, transforming our understanding of humankind's place in the universe more thoroughly than did the old astro-futurism. The end of the Cold War was accompanied by the rise of global warming. The years 1988–92 brought the Earth Summit, global citizenship, NASA's "Mission to Earth," and new and more distant views of the home planet Earth as a "Pale blue dot." . . .

Confidence in the progress of science and technology was never higher than at the time of the first journeys to the Moon; afterwards came the first "Earth Day," the crisis of confidence and the environmentalist renaissance. At the very apex of human progress the question was asked, "Where next?" and the answer came, "Home." Earthrise was an epiphany in space.

The Apollo Space Program Accelerated Development of Computer Technology

Sharon Gaudin

In the following viewpoint, Sharon Gaudin describes how the the advances in technology necessary for the Apollo moon program had a major impact on the development of products taken for granted today. For example, computers of the 1950s and 1960s were room-sized machines that used a lot of electric power, but for going to the moon they had to be made small and light-weight, with low power requirements. Integrated circuits were developed for this purpose, and all electronic equipment today depends on them. By now, they have become microchips and without them such things as cell phones and laptops could not exist. Various technologies were developed as a direct result of the Apollo program's requirements and might never have been

SOURCE. Sharon Gaudin, "NASA's Apollo Technology Has Changed History," www.computerworld.com, August 12, 2010. Copyright © 2009 by Computerworld. All rights reserved. Reproduced by permission.

made without the funding supplied by NASA. Gaudin is a senior writer at *Computerworld* magazine.

Forty years after astronauts on NASA'S Apollo 11 spacecraft first landed on the moon, many experts say the historic event altered the course of space exploration as well man's view of itself in the universe.

The Apollo missions also had another major affect on the world—rapidly accelerating the pace of technology development. The work of NASA engineers at the time caused a dramatic shift in electronics and computing systems, scientists say.

Without the research and development that went into those space missions, top companies like Intel Corp. may not have been founded, and the population likely wouldn't be spending a big chunk of work and free time using laptops and Blackberries to post information on Facebook or Twitter.

"During the mid- to late-1960s, when Apollo was being designed and built, there was significant advancement," said Scott Hubbard, who worked at NASA for 20 years before joining the faculty at Stanford University, where he is a professor in the aeronautics and astronautics department. "Power consumption. Mass. Volume. Data rate. All the things that were important to making space flight feasible led to major changes in technology. A little told story is how much NASA, from the Cold War up through the late '80s or early '90s affected technology."

It's fairly well-known that technology developed by NASA scientists routinely makes its way into products developed in the robotics, computer hardware and software, nanotech-

'There were remarkable discoveries in civil, electrical, aeronautical and engineering science, as well as rocketry and the development of core technologies that really pushed technology into the industry it is today.'

nology, aeronautics, transportation and health care industries. While the story that Tang, the bright orange powdered beverage, was developed for astronauts is just a myth, many other advancements—think microelectromechanical systems, supercomputers and microcomputers, software and microprocessors—were also created using technology developed by NASA over the past half century.

Hubbard noted that overall, $7 or $8 in goods and services are still produced for every $1 that the government invests in NASA.

But the string of Apollo missions alone—which ran from the ill-fated, never-flown Apollo 1 mission in 1967 to Apollo 17, the last to land men on the moon, in 1972—had a critical, and often overlooked impact on technology at a key time in the computer industry.

Daniel Lockney, the editor of *Spinoff*, NASA's annual publication that reports on the use of the agency's technologies in the private sector, said the advancements during the Apollo missions were staggering.

"There were remarkable discoveries in civil, electrical, aeronautical and engineering science, as well as rocketry and the development of core technologies that really pushed technology into the industry it is today," he said. "It was perhaps one of the greatest engineering and scientific feats of all time. It was huge. The engineering required to leave Earth and move to another heavenly body required the development of new technologies that before hadn't even been thought of. It has yet to be rivaled."

Lockney cited several technologies that can be directly linked engineering work done for the Apollo missions.

Software designed to manage a complex series of systems onboard the capsules is an ancestor to the software that today is used in retail credit card swipe devices, he said. And race car drivers and firefighters today use

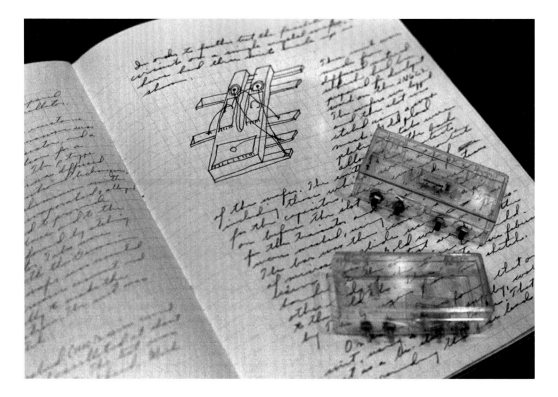

The integrated circuit, which Jack Kilby invented to make computers feasible aboard NASA spacecraft, was a precursor to chip technology. (Paul Buck/ AFP/Getty Images.)

liquid-cooled garments based on the devices created for Apollo astronauts to wear under their spacesuits. And the freeze-dried foods developed for Apollo astronauts to eat in space are used today in military field rations, known as MREs, and as part of survival gear.

And those technologies are just a drop in the bucket to importance of the development of the integrated circuit, and the emergence of Silicon Valley, which were very closely linked to the Apollo program.

The development of that integrated circuit, the forbearer to the microchip, basically is a miniaturized electronic circuit that did away with the manual assembly of separate transistors and capacitors. Revolutionizing electronics, integrated circuits are used in nearly all electronic equipment today.

While Robert Noyce, co-founder of Fairchild Semiconductor and then Intel Corp. is credited with cofounding the microchip, Jack Kilby of Texas Instruments demonstrated the first working integrated circuit that was built for the U.S. Department of Defense and NASA.

NASA, according to Lockney, set the parameters of what it needed out of the technology and then Kilby designed it. Kilby later won the Nobel Prize in Physics for for creating the technology.

"The co-investment between defense and civilian space was very real and hugely important," said Hubbard.

"With Apollo, they needed to cut down on weight and power consumption. Mass into space equals money," he said. "It has been and continues to be about $10,000 a pound to get to lower Earth orbit. They certainly don't want computers that take up basketball courts. They want something very powerful and very light that doesn't take massive power. That was one of the driving requirements that led to the development of the integrated circuit, where you put all the components on a chip rather than having a board stuffed with individual transistors and other circuit components."

He added that the microchip took the high-tech industry to a place of mass production and economies of scale.

"There was a major shift in electronics and computing and at least half credit goes to Apollo," said Hubbard. "Without it, you wouldn't have a laptop. You'd still have things like the Univac."

The Apollo Space Program Inspired Young People to Choose Technological Careers

S. Alan Stern

In the following viewpoint, a former NASA administrator declares that, although the Apollo moon program accomplished many important things, its greatest achievement in his opinion was the inspiration it provided to young people of the baby boom generation. Many of these young people chose scientific or technical careers and have since transformed the economy of the United States with their innovations, producing a return many times greater than the $100-plus billion investment in going to the moon. S. Alan Stern is a planetary scientist, writer, and speaker.

SOURCE. S. Alan Stern, "Apollo's Greatest Achievement," www.thespacereview.com, first published by *Space News*, August 12, 2010. Copyright © 2009 by S. Alan Stern. All rights reserved. Reproduced by permission.

I was born the year of Sputnik [the first space satellite, launched by the Soviet Union in 1957] and my earliest memories of society swirl around silver suited astronauts and the promise of a bright future of gleaming spaceships and planetary homesteading. When I was 11, some 40 years ago this month, America's Apollo program achieved something so much larger than life—President [John F.] Kennedy's goal of "landing a man on the Moon, and returning him safely to Earth"—that it seemed that future was already upon us.

Now, looking back as we celebrate that singularly human, and singularly historic achievement—journeying to and walking on another world—we know that the 2009 I imagined as a boy is oh so different from the real 2009 we live in. It's so different, in fact, that people even wonder if Apollo was worth the cost, and if it was more than a historical footnote—an odd bit of the distant future that took early but only short-lived root in the middle of the 20th century.

So today, as we take stock of Apollo 40 years later, is a good time to ask what each of us thinks the greatest impact of the $100+ billion Apollo project really was.

The long ballyhooed achievements of Apollo are many. There is the Cold War propaganda victory that came with wave after wave of international accolades for America. There is the internal boost that Apollo's success provided at a time when assassinations, race riots, student strife, and an unpopular war were the norm. There is the transformative awareness of the Earth as a finite planetary oasis in the vast and hostile ocean of space. They also include scientific discoveries that revolutionized our understanding of the origin of the Moon, the evolution of planetary crusts, and chronology of our home solar system. And they include revolutionary advances in electronics technology that fueled revolutions in telecommunications and computing that have transformed how we live and work. Each

THE SIX MOON LANDINGS

Mission	Landing date	Astronauts	Command module	Lunar lander	Landing site
Apollo 11	July 20, 1969	Neil Armstrong Buzz Aldrin Michael Collins	Columbia	Eagle	Mare Tranquillitatis
Apollo 12	Nov. 19, 1969	Pete Conrad Dick Gordon Alan Bean	Yankee Clipper	Intrepid	Oceanus Procellarum
Apollo 14	Feb. 5, 1971	Alan Shepard Stuart Roosa Edgar Mitchell	Kitty Hawk	Antares	Fra Mauro
Apollo 15	July 30, 1971	David Scott James Irwin Alfred Worden	Endeavour	Falcon	Hadley Rille
Apollo 16	Apr. 20, 1972	John Young Ken Mattingly Charles Duke	Casper	Orion	Descartes
Apollo 17	Dec. 11, 1972	Eugene Cernan Ron Evans Harrison Schmitt	America	Challenger	Taurus-Littrow

Compiled by editor.

of these achievements has been cited as being worthy of Apollo's cost.

Apollo's Greatest Achievement

But in my view, the greatest achievement of Apollo is something more important, something that took decades to be recognized, and which is only now coming into focus.

As I see it, the greatest achievement of Apollo is the inspiration that Apollo's bold, quickly-paced, and futuristic accomplishment generated in so many baby boomers, whose hearts were captured by the tsunami of new technologies Apollo generated and the sheer exuberance for invention that space exploration inspired.

> The children and adolescents whose hearts were stirred and minds were captured by Apollo's inspiration number in the millions.

As a result, armies of kids like myself followed their hearts, stirred by the epic, larger-than-life explorations of Apollo that unfolded before them on TVs, and chose careers in computer science, electrical engineering, aerospace engineering, geophysics, and a dozen other technical fields. The children and adolescents whose hearts were stirred and minds were captured by Apollo's inspiration number in the millions, and include names then like Paul Allen, Jeff Bezos, Sergey Brin, John Carmack, Bill Gates, Steve Jobs, and Elon Musk, all captains of the computing and Internet revolutions.

When these and others of Apollo's children entered the workforce, we thoroughly transformed our economy and lives in ways virtually no one could have imagined 40 years ago. We did so by sparking a bevy of tech revolutions that showered society with inventions, productivity increases, and new ways of socializing across the '80s, '90s, and this decade too. This—a trillion-dollar dividend for a $100+ billion investment—is truly Apollo's best achievement, its best spinoff.

Computing innovators Steve Jobs and Bill Gates were among the young people who felt the influence of the moon landing. (Andy Freeberg.)

And this very special dividend continues to generate good return even today. Some of the most successful "children of Apollo" are now returning to their space roots, investing their time and their fortunes to open up space exploration in wholly new and imaginative ways with private companies like Armadillo Aerospace, Blue Origin, SpaceX, and Virgin Galactic. Indeed, perhaps in another 10 years, the second greatest achievement of Apollo will be seen as the space access revolution that baby boomer tech billionaires are now giving birth to. But I digress.

President [Barack] Obama's administration is now taking up the reins of our national space program and choosing its forward course. As this young and innovative administration shapes America's civil space program, I hope they will fashion a bold, innovative, and quickly paced 21st century effort of equally stirring nature to

Apollo. For if they do, they can expect its cost to be repaid many times over, as Apollo's was, by the children and teens inspired to take up technical fields, fueling our economy, and revolutionizing life for the better, across the next 40 years.

The Moon Landing Showed That the Future of Earth Is Global

Jean-Jacques Dordain

In the following question-and-answer article, Jean-Jacques Dordain, the director general of the European Space Agency, discusses the significance of the Apollo 11 moon landing on its fortieth anniversary. Dr. Dordain says that it no longer matters that it was a competition between the United States and the Soviet Union. It is more important now that the sight of Earth from space showed us that our planet's future is global. He is sure that humans will someday go back to the moon for scientific discovery, to use its resources, or to establish a warning system against asteroids, and that developing technology for recycling resources on the moon will affect the way resources are used on Earth. The moon and Mars are part of humankind's environment, he declares, and the long-term future of humankind cannot be thought of as if Earth were in isolation.

SOURCE. Jean-Jacques Dordain, "ESA's Director General on Apollo 11 Anniversary," www.esa.int, July 28, 2010. Copyright © 2009 by European Space Agency. All rights reserved. Reproduced by permission.

*F*orty years ago, man first set foot on the Moon. What did that signify?

Back then, it meant that US technology was stronger than Soviet technology, because it was the US flag that was planted on the Moon. But today, I think we can see this in a totally different light. The fact that it was a US flag is no longer what matters most.

I think the most important thing, and what will be remembered far longer, is that astronauts discovered planet Earth; they saw Earth resembling a small 'blue marble' floating in the Universe. They were able to bring back to Earth the notion that our future is a global one and that we have to think about the future of Earth globally, and not individually. So this is what it means today, which is very different from what it meant 40 years ago.

> It seems to me that the Moon is simply a part of our environment and I am sure humans will return to the Moon.

Will mankind go back to the Moon? If so, when and how?

Yes, I am sure mankind will go back to the Moon. The Moon is just three days away from Earth, and it used to take three days to go from Paris to Marseille a little over a hundred years ago, so I don't see why we shouldn't go back to the Moon. However, the aim would no longer be to plant a flag there.

The idea would be to use the Moon as just another part of our environment, in order to make scientific progress, or to establish a warning system against asteroids or anything else threatening Earth, or as a source of resources to take back to Earth. It seems to me that the Moon is simply a part of our environment and I am sure humans will return to the Moon; but they will go to the Moon together and not in the context of two competing countries.

Will Europe go to the Moon?

The European Space Agency has sent dozens of payloads into orbit—like this Ariane-4 rocket carrying an international telecommunications satellite. A lunar mission may be in the organization's future. (**Arianespace/AP Images.**)

I think Europe will play a part in the international exploration of the Moon; but with what means, we don't yet know. That is a choice to be made at a political level, not at agency level. Because the fact is that Europe today is dependent on others to go to the Moon with astronauts. And since we are dependent, we cannot take any initiatives. We can only contribute to a US-led exploration programme.

Europe can certainly bring some interesting technologies to areas where I would say we are the best in the world, but no initiative-taking would be involved. So that is the first scenario: a European contribution to a US-led exploration programme.

> Planet Earth is not isolated and we cannot think about its future in total isolation.

However, there is a second scenario, which would be for Europe to build up the capabilities to take initiatives. But that is a very different scenario, because it would first of all require developing new capabilities, in particular a crew transportation system. This would call for a high-level political decision, as well as discussions at political level about Europe's position in a lunar exploration programme.

When? In my view, this mainly depends on the current US plan. . . . I would say, though, that the date is not the most important factor. We're not talking about a race anymore, which means that we have time. If it's not in 2020, it will be in 2025—it doesn't really matter.

In a hundred years from now, nobody will worry whether we returned to the Moon in 2020 or 2025, and that is why we at ESA [European Space Agency] are giving far more priority to science and short-term services to citizens. However, I am absolutely convinced that mankind will go back to the Moon—in 10 years' time, or maybe 20 years, but that is not the important point.

But where it is difficult to find the money, why spend it on the Moon?

For several reasons, first because the long-term future of Earth cannot be considered without taking into account our environment, and the Moon and Mars are part of our environment. Planet Earth is not isolated and we cannot think about its future in total isolation. So the first reason is to prepare for the long term.

The second reason is to develop innovative technologies: to go to the Moon, we shall have to develop a lot of technologies that are not yet available, for example, the recycling of resources. We cannot take to the Moon every litre of water, every litre of oxygen and every kilogram of food that the astronauts will need to live there.

This means that we will have to recycle resources on the Moon as much as possible to produce water and oxygen and grow plants. And these types of technology, which we are working on right now and which are necessary for a lunar base, will have a lot of consequences in terms of the way we use resources on Earth.

And the third reason: we need to provide younger generations with challenging projects to make sure we attract the best talents to science and engineering. Unfortunately, in most developed countries, gifted young people are showing a lack of interest in these fields, but I am convinced that this type of project can help attract them to science and engineering.

Where were you when Apollo 11 landed on the Moon and what were your thoughts?

I remember very clearly where I was, I spent the night in front of my TV. I also recall getting my engineering degree on 20 July at noon. I was an engineer, and to celebrate, I went on vacation. That night I was in the southwest of France in a very small village watching TV.

At the time it seemed like a dream to me, a technological achievement, and I am not too sure that I appreciated all the implications of what I was living through. I think I just enjoyed the event without learning too many lessons from it. But at the very same time I became an engineer able to work in the space field, and here I now am, still in space!

The Arguments of Moon Landing Deniers Are Based on Ignorance of Science

Mike Hall

The following viewpoint explains that the belief that the moon landings were faked is based on ignorance of scientific facts. The writer lists the claims made in an article in the British newspaper the *Telegraph*, which presented the hoax theory as if it were true, and he tells why each of them is invalid. Besides being contrary to basic science, some of the claims involve a lack of knowledge of what special effects would be possible to produce in a film today, let alone forty years ago. Mike Hall is the founder and president of the Merseyside Skeptics Society, a British nonprofit organization that seeks to determine the truth or falsehood of scientific and historical claims by examining the evidence.

SOURCE. Mike Hall, "10 Reasons the *Telegraph* Needs a Science Writer," www.merseyskeptics.org.uk, October 4, 2010. Copyright © 2009 by Mike Hall. All rights reserved. Reproduced by permission.

This week [July 2009] being the 40th anniversary of the Apollo 11 mission, it isn't really surprising that the Moon Landing Deniers [MLD] are getting some coverage in the press. Not in the *Telegraph*, however. To mark this historic occasion, a newspaper with less self discipline might have printed a puff piece for an MLD group; or perhaps ran an uncritical interview with some conspiracy nut. But not the *Telegraph*, no. They cut out the middle man and print the Moon Hoax story as if it were fact.

Cheers, guys.

One at a time then.

When the astronauts are putting up the American flag it waves. There is no wind on the Moon.

No, it doesn't. There, that was easy . . . this debunking lark is a piece of cake, isn't it? No? What do you mean you need more detail than that? Oh, okay, okay fine.

They're right to say there is no wind on the moon. That's because there is no atmosphere. With no atmosphere, there is no drag. You might remember this one from school, when your teacher dropped a feather and a piece of lead in a vacuum. With no air, no drag to slow the feather down, they fall at the same rate.

What people interpret as the flag "waving" is actually the flag swaying from the momentum of being adjusted by the astronauts as they put it up. With no drag to slow it down, a flag will keep oscillating like this for quite a while—giving the impression of it waving in a non-existent breeze.

No stars are visible in the pictures taken by the Apollo astronauts from the surface of the Moon.

There are no stars outside my window when I look up at the sky now either. That's because it's 2.30 in the afternoon. It's no different on the Moon; there are no stars because it is day time. With no atmosphere to scatter the light, the sky on the Moon remains black during the day, but the Sun still produces enough light to drown out the stars. If the camera shutter had been left open long enough for the stars to be visible, then everything else would have been ridiculously over-exposed.

No blast crater is visible in the pictures taken of the lunar landing module.

Who says there should be a blast crater? As the lander descended, there was only around one-and-a-half pounds per square inch of thrust coming off the rockets. That's not a lot of pressure. Plus, there is no atmosphere on the Moon. Any exhaust from the rockets will dissipate very quickly, not billow like it would on Earth. There is no blast crater because there wasn't enough pressure hitting the ground to produce one.

The landing module weighs 17 tons and yet sits on top of the sand making no impression. Next to it astronauts' footprints can be seen in the sand.

Actually, the lander would have weighed less than three tons on the Moon—one-sixth gravity and all that—but that's beside the point. It's not weight that determines the depth of the impression one leaves in the lunar regolith, it's pressure. Although the lander was much heavier than the astronauts, its weight was spread across the four, one-metre wide landing pads. The weight of the astronauts, on the other hand, was concentrated on to the soles of their relatively tiny boots.

> The only way to achieve [the lunar dust movement] effect would be to put the entire sound stage in a vacuum—something we'd struggle to do today, much less 40 years ago!

The footprints in the fine lunar dust, with no moisture or atmosphere or strong gravity, are unexpectedly well preserved, as if made in wet sand.

Who didn't expect them to be well preserved? You? That's a clear argument from ignorance. Again, the Moon has no atmosphere, thus no weather. With nothing to weather rocks, the lunar regolith isn't smooth and rounded, like Earth sand, it's jagged and spikey. The

An Unmanned Spacecraft Has Photographed the Moon Landing Sites

In the summer of 2009, the unmanned Lunar Reconnaissance Orbiter (LRO) took photographs showing all six moon landing sites, including lunar modules, some astronaut footprints, and tracks of the lunar rover that was used on the last three Apollo missions. This evidence should put any doubts about their existence to rest, but since it is not widely known, a small percentage of the public still thinks that all twelve of the astronauts who walked on the moon—plus the many scientists throughout the world who have examined lunar data—have been lying.

The purpose of sending the LRO to the moon was not to prove that humans had landed there. Its goal, according to NASA, was "to create a comprehensive atlas of the Moon's features and resources to aid in the design of a lunar outpost." (At the time, a future return to the moon was officially planned, although in early 2010 President Barack Obama decided against this in favor of preparation for eventual trips to the asteroids and Mars.) The data gathered "will provide a deeper understanding of the moon and its environment," NASA's LRO Fact

spikes lock together like a dry stone wall, holding the impression of the footprint in place. Next!

When the landing module takes off from the Moon's surface there is no visible flame from the rocket.

That's right. So? Oh, I see. You think there *should* be a flame? Well, you're wrong. The fuels used by the landing module, hydrazine and dinitrogen tetroxide, don't produce a visible flame. That's why you can't see one.

Impossible Camera Tricks

If you speed up the film of the astronauts walking on the Moon's surface they look like they were filmed on Earth and slowed down.

The excellent [television show] *Mythbusters* recently spent some time trying to recreate the "look" of the

Sheet stated. "This will clear the way for a safe human return to the Moon and for future human exploration of our solar system."

As of 2010, the major discovery made by the LRO is that the landing sites are not representative of the whole moon and that it has far more resources than scientists had believed. In the fall of 2009 researchers announced that water had been found there through the deliberate crashing of the LRO's companion spacecraft LCROSS (Lunar Crater Observation and Sensing Satellite), which sent up a plume of dust and vapor that provided data for analysis. The October 22, 2010, issue of the journal *Science* reported that some areas of the moon have more water (in the form of ice crystals) than the Sahara desert on Earth. Hydrogen and traces of other important elements, even silver and gold, have also been found. Conceivably, the moon's resources could supply a lunar base with air, drinking water, and rocket fuel, and some people feel that the decision against building one should, therefore, be reevaluated.

Moon's low-gravity environment using camera tricks and special effects. They had Adam Savage bounce around in a space suit, messed with the frame rate, hoisted him up on wires . . . every trick they could think of. The only way they found to make him move the way astronauts do was by putting him in a vomit comet [an aircraft that can simulate low gravity] and actually shooting in one-sixth gravity.

Even assuming that, somehow, in the 1960s they found a way to use camera tricks to simulate the low-gravity look of the footage—that doesn't explain the moon rover. As it moves around, you can see the lunar dust being thrown up by the rover's wheels in perfect parabolas. On Earth, the dust would billow out from the wheels, like Jeremy Clarkson in the Mojave Desert. The

only way to achieve this effect would be to put the entire sound stage in a vacuum—something we'd struggle to do today, much less 40 years ago!

The astronauts could not have survived the trip because of exposure to radiation from the Van Allen radiation belt.

Contrary to what you may have heard in *Doctor Who and the Silurians*, the Van Allen belt is not the same thing as the ozone layer. The Van Allen belt is actually a belt of charged particles around the Earth, held in place by Earth's magnetic field.

It's true that an unprotected astronaut would not survive too long when exposed to the radiation in the Van Allen belt—but then the astronauts on Apollo 11 weren't unprotected. They had a whacking great

> If there was a conspiracy to fake the Moon landing, the Russians were in on it. Not very likely in the middle of the Cold War.

tin can around them called a *space ship* which blocked out most of the radiation. Apollo 11 would [have] been through the Van Allen belt and out the other side in an hour or so. There wasn't enough radiation exposure, or enough time, to cause anyone any harm.

The rocks brought back from the Moon are identical to rocks collected by scientific expeditions to Antarctica.

Depends on which rocks you're talking about, and what you mean by identical. Lunar meteorites—bits of the Moon that have been ejected and then crashed on Earth—have been found in Antarctica. And so, to that extent, "identical" rocks have been collected by scientific expeditions to Antarctica. However, these rocks were not discovered until 1979 and weren't recognised as lunar rocks until 1982. They're also very rare. How NASA is supposed to have recovered 300 kilos of them, 10 years before anyone knew they existed, is beyond me.

There are no scientific accounts published in peer-reviewed journals disputing the origin of the rocks

Photo on opposite page: Neil Armstrong took this photo of Buzz Aldrin on the moon. Stars are invisible in the moon's black, daytime "sky," as they are in the blue skies of Earth by day. (Apic/Getty Images.)

retrieved by the Apollo missions. The rock also matches the rocks later recovered by the Soviets so, if there was a conspiracy to fake the Moon landing, the Russians were in on it. Not very likely in the middle of the Cold War.

Why No One Has Returned to the Moon

All six Moon landings happened during the [President Richard] Nixon administration. No other national leader has claimed to have landed astronauts on the Moon, despite 40 years of rapid technological development.

> The reason no other national leader has claimed to land astronauts on the Moon is because no other nation has!

This is a new one on me, I have to admit. I'm not entirely sure what they're trying to say? Some attempt at poisoning the well, perhaps? Nixon was a crook, therefore the Moon landings never happened? Sorry guys, I'm afraid that's a complete non-sequitur. The reason no other national leader has claimed to land astronauts on the Moon is because no other nation has!

As for why that is, I think it's because the political will hasn't been there. After the Soviets put [cosmonaut Yuri] Gagarin into space, [John F.] Kennedy wasn't going to sit there and let them be first to the Moon as well. This gave a huge political impetus to the whole affair. Not because they are easy, but because they are hard, etc. There was money and talent being thrown at the fledgling NASA.

There have always been a million scientific reasons why people should return to the Moon but, from a political perspective, what would be the point? Who is there to beat? Uncle Sam has been resting on his laurels.

Happily, it looks like that is changing. With the US looking to the Moon and then Mars, it's exciting times for space fans!

So there you have it . . . and if I could work that up in the space of a couple of hours, I don't understand why the *Telegraph* can't?

Update. To their credit, the *Telegraph* have now added a video to the article, which goes through many of the common MLD claims and debunks them.

America's Retreat from the Moon Is Unwise and Unnecessary

Charles Krauthammer

In the following viewpoint, Charles Krauthammer expresses his dismay at the United States' abandonment of the moon program—a development which would have seemed incredible to anyone in the past who was told that travel to the moon would someday become possible. Nothing of significance has been done in space during the past forty years, he says. The space shuttle is a beautiful machine but its potential has been wasted, and when it is retired, the United States will be incapable even of reaching low orbit. Although there are problems on Earth that going back to the moon would not solve, humans did not go there for practical reasons in the first place. The purpose of exploration, he declares, is to open possibilities that cannot be foreseen—such as the photo of Earth from the moon that led to environmental consciousness, but which, ironically, turned the public's imagination away from space. In his opinion, retreat

SOURCE. Charles Krauthammer, "The Moon We Left Behind," www.washingtonpost.com, July 23, 2010. Copyright © 2009 by Washington Post. All rights reserved. Reproduced by permission.

from adventure was tragically wrong. Krauthammer is a nationally syndicated political columnist.

Michael Crichton once wrote that if you told a physicist in 1899 that within a hundred years humankind would, among other wonders (nukes, commercial airlines), "travel to the moon, and then lose interest . . . the physicist would almost certainly pronounce you mad." In 2000, I quoted these lines expressing Crichton's incredulity at America's abandonment of the moon. It is now 2009 and the moon recedes ever further.

Next week marks the 40th anniversary of the first moon landing [in 1969]. We say we will return in 2020. But that promise was made by a previous president, and this president has defined himself as the antimatter to George [W.] Bush. Moreover, for all of Barack Obama's Kennedyesque qualities, he has expressed none of [John F.] Kennedy's enthusiasm for human space exploration.

So with the Apollo moon program long gone, and with Constellation, its supposed successor, still little more than a hope, we remain in retreat from space. Astonishing. After countless millennia of gazing and dreaming, we finally got off the ground at Kitty Hawk in 1903. Within 66 years, a nanosecond in human history, we'd landed on the moon. Then five more landings, 10 more moonwalkers and, in the decades since, nothing.

> Social ills will always be with us. If we'd waited for them to be rectified before venturing out, we'd still be living in caves.

To be more precise: almost 40 years spent in low Earth orbit studying, well, zero-G nausea and sundry cosmic mysteries. We've done it with the most beautiful, intricate, complicated—and ultimately, hopelessly impractical—machine ever built by man: the space shuttle. We turned this magnificent bird into a truck for hauling goods and people to a tinkertoy we call the international space station, itself created in a fit of post-Cold War internationalist absentmindedness as a place where people of differing nationality can sing "Kumbaya" while weightless.

> When you do such magnificently hard things—send sailing a Ferdinand Magellan or a Neil Armstrong—you open new human possibility in ways utterly unpredictable.

The shuttle is now too dangerous, too fragile and too expensive. Seven more flights and then it is retired, going—like [heavy transport aircraft prototype] the Spruce Goose and [supersonic jet] the Concorde—into the Museum of Things Too Beautiful and Complicated to Survive.

America's manned space program is in shambles. Fourteen months from today, for the first time since 1962, the United States will be incapable not just of sending a man to the moon but of sending anyone into Earth orbit. We'll be totally grounded. We'll have to beg a ride from the Russians or perhaps even the Chinese.

Now Is the Time to Return to the Moon

So what, you say? Don't we have problems here on Earth? Oh, please. Poverty and disease and social ills will always be with us. If we'd waited for them to be rectified before venturing out, we'd still be living in caves.

Yes, we have a financial crisis. No one's asking for a crash Manhattan Project [the all-out effort that produced the atomic bomb]. All we need is sufficient funding from the hundreds of billions being showered from Washington—"stimulus" monies that, unlike [President Dwight D.] Eisenhower's Interstate highway system or Kennedy's Apollo program, will leave behind not a trace on our country or our consciousness—to build Constellation and get us back to Earth orbit and the moon a half-century after the original landing.

Why do it? It's not for practicality. We didn't go to the moon to spin off cooling suits and freeze-dried fruit. Any technological return is a bonus, not a reason. We go for the wonder and glory of it. Or, to put it less grandly, for its immense possibilities. We choose to do such things, said JFK, "not because they are easy, but because they are hard." And when you do such magnificently hard things—send sailing a Ferdinand Magellan or a Neil Armstrong—you open new human possibility in ways utterly unpredictable.

The greatest example? Who could have predicted that the moon voyages would create the most potent impetus to—and symbol of—environmental consciousness here on Earth: Earthrise, the now iconic Blue Planet photograph brought back by Apollo 8?

Ironically, that new consciousness about the uniqueness and fragility of Earth focused contemporary imagination away from space and back to Earth. We are now deep into that hyper-terrestrial phase, the

As of 2008, key elements of NASA's Constellation program, like the Orion crew module seen here, remained stalled in the development stage. (**Paul J. Richards/ AFP/Getty Images.**)

age of iPod and Facebook, of social networking and eco-consciousness.

But look up from your BlackBerry one night. That is the moon. On it are exactly 12 sets of human footprints—untouched, unchanged, abandoned. For the first time in history, the moon is not just a mystery and a muse, but a nightly rebuke. A vigorous young president once summoned us to this new frontier, calling the voyage "the most hazardous and dangerous and greatest adventure on which man has ever embarked." And so we did it. We came. We saw. Then we retreated.

How could we?

CHAPTER 3

Personal Narratives

The Astronauts Describe the Moon Landing

NASA

In the following excerpt from a NASA account of the first moon landing, astronauts Neil Armstrong, Buzz Aldrin, and Michael Collins tell what it was like to descend onto the surface and what they did when they got there. They found that they liked moving around in the moon's low gravity and the scenery was beautiful, though desolate. But they were too busy for sightseeing, as they had more things to do than there was time for. The only thing that they had difficulty with was getting the flag to stay up. Before they left, the President of the United States talked to them in what he called the most historical phone call ever made.

Photo on previous page: An artist's rendering shows Apollo 11's lunar module departing the moon to return the astronauts home to Earth. (Pierre Mion/ National Geographic/ Getty Images.)

NEIL ARMSTRONG: In the final phases of the descent after a number of program alarms, we looked at the landing area and found a very large crater. This is the area we decided we would not go into;

SOURCE. "Chapter 11.4," *Apollo Expeditions to the Moon*, edited by Edgar M. Cortright. NASA, 1975.

we extended the range downrange. The exhaust dust was kicked up by the engine and this caused some concern in that it degraded our ability to determine not only our altitude in the final phases but also our translational velocities over the ground. It's quite important not to stub your toe during the final phases of touchdown.

From the Space-to-Ground Tapes

EAGLE [landing craft]: 540 feet, down at 30 [feet per second] . . . down at 15 . . . 400 feet down at 9 . . . forward . . . 350 feet, down at 4 . . . 300 feet, down 3 1/2 . . . 47 forward . . . 1 1/2 down . . . 13 forward . . . 11 forward? coming down nicely . . . 200 feet, 4 1/2 down . . . 5 1/2 down . . . 5 percent . . . 75 feet . . . 6 forward . . . lights on . . . down 2 1/2 . . . 40 feet? down 2 1/2, kicking up some dust . . . 30 feet, 2 1/2 down . . . faint shadow . . . 4 forward . . . 4 forward . . . drifting to right a little . . . O.K. . . .

HOUSTON [Mission Control Center]: 30 seconds [fuel remaining].

EAGLE: Contact light! O.K., engine stop . . . descent engine command override off . . .

HOUSTON: We copy you down, Eagle.

EAGLE: Houston, Tranquility Base here. The Eagle has landed!

HOUSTON: Roger, Tranquility. We copy you on the ground. You've got a bunch of guys about to turn blue. We're breathing again. Thanks a lot.

TRANQUILITY [moon landing site]: Thank you . . . That may have seemed like a very long final phase. The auto targeting was taking us right into a football-field-sized crater, with a large number of big boulders and rocks for about one or two crater-diameters around it, and it required flying

> "We felt very comfortable in the lunar gravity. It was, in fact, in our view preferable both to weightlessness and to the Earth's gravity."

manually over the rock field to find a reasonably good area.

HOUSTON: Roger, we copy. It was beautiful from here, Tranquility. Over.

TRANQUILITY: We'll get to the details of what's around here, but it looks like a collection of just about every variety of shape, angularity, granularity, about every variety of rock you could find.

HOUSTON: Roger, Tranquility. Be advised there's lots of smiling faces in this room, and all over the world.

TRANQUILITY: There are two of them up here.

COLUMBIA [command module]: And don't forget one in the command module.

Stepping Onto the Moon's Surface

ARMSTRONG: Once [we] settled on the surface, the dust settled immediately and we had an excellent view of the area surrounding the LM [lunar module]. We saw a crater surface, pockmarked with craters up to 15, 20, 30 feet, and many smaller craters down to a diameter of 1 foot and, of course, the surface was very fine-grained. There were a surprising number of rocks of all sizes.

A number of experts had, prior to the flight, predicted that a good bit of difficulty might be encountered by people due to the variety of strange atmospheric and gravitational characteristics. This didn't prove to be the case and after landing we felt very comfortable in the lunar gravity. It was, in fact, in our view preferable both to weightlessness and to the Earth's gravity.

> The primary difficulty was just far too little time to do the variety of things we would have liked.

When we actually descended the ladder it was found to be very much like the lunar-gravity simulations we had performed here on Earth. No difficulty was encountered in descending the ladder. The last step was about 3 1/2 feet from the surface, and we were somewhat concerned that we might have difficulty in reentering the LM at the end of our activity period. So we practiced that before bringing the camera down.

BUZZ ALDRIN: We opened the hatch and Neil, with me as his navigator, began backing out of the tiny opening. It seemed like a small eternity before I heard Neil say, "That's one small step for man . . . one giant leap for mankind." In less than fifteen minutes I was backing awkwardly out of the hatch and onto the surface to join Neil, who, in the tradition of all tourists, had his camera ready to photograph my arrival.

I felt buoyant and full of goose pimples when I stepped down on the surface. I immediately looked down at my feet and became intrigued with the peculiar properties of the lunar dust. If one kicks sand on a beach, it scatters in numerous directions with some grains traveling farther than others. On the Moon the dust travels exactly and precisely as it goes in various directions, and every grain of it lands nearly the same distance away.

The Boy in the Candy Store

ARMSTRONG: There were a lot of things to do, and we had a hard time getting them finished. We had very little trouble, much less trouble than expected, on the surface. It was a pleasant operation. Temperatures weren't high. They were very comfortable. The little EMU, the combination of spacesuit and backpack that sustained our life on the surface, operated magnificently. The primary difficulty was just far too little time to do the variety of things we would have liked. We had the problem of the five-year-old boy in a candy store.

ALDRIN: I took off jogging to test my maneuverability. The exercise gave me an odd sensation and looked even more odd when I later saw the films of it. With bulky suits on, we

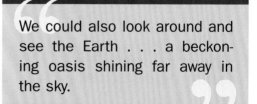

We could also look around and see the Earth . . . a beckoning oasis shining far away in the sky.

Neil Armstrong, Buzz Aldrin, and Michael Collins (left to right) were awarded the Langley Gold Medal for aviation at the Smithsonian Air and Space Museum on the 30th anniversary of the first landing on the moon. (Doug Mills/AP Images.)

seemed to be moving in slow motion. I noticed immediately that my inertia seemed much greater. Earth-bound, I would have stopped my run in just one step, but I had to use three of four steps to sort of wind down. My Earth weight, with the big backpack and heavy suit, was 360 pounds. On the Moon I weighed only 60 pounds.

At one point I remarked that the surface was "Beautiful, beautiful. Magnificent desolation." I was struck by the contrast between the starkness of the shadows and the desert-like barrenness of the rest of the surface. It ranged from dusty gray to light tan and was unchanging except for one startling sight: our LM sitting there with its black, silver, and bright yellow-orange thermal coating shining brightly in the otherwise colorless landscape. I had seen Neil in his suit thousands of times before, but on the Moon the unnatural whiteness of it seemed unusually brilliant. We could also look around and see the Earth, which, though much larger than the Moon the Earth was seeing, seemed small—a beckoning oasis shining far away in the sky.

As the sequence of lunar operations evolved, Neil had the camera most of the time, and the majority of pictures taken on the Moon that include an astronaut are of me. It wasn't until we were back on Earth and in the Lunar Receiving Laboratory looking over the pictures that we realized there were few pictures of Neil. My fault perhaps, but we had never simulated this in our training.

Coaxing the Flag to Stand

During a pause in experiments, Neil suggested we proceed with the flag. It took both of us to set it up and it was nearly a disaster. Public Relations obviously needs practice just as everything else does. A small telescoping arm was attached to the flagpole to keep the flag extended and perpendicular. As hard as we tried, the telescope wouldn't fully extend. Thus the flag which should have been flat, had its own unique permanent wave. Then to our dismay the staff of the pole wouldn't go far enough into the lunar surface to support itself in an upright position. After much struggling we finally coaxed it to remain upright, but in a most precarious position. I dreaded the possibility of the American flag collapsing into the lunar dust in front of the television camera.

MICHAEL COLLINS [on his fourth orbital pass above]: "How's it going?" "The EVA is progressing beautifully. I believe they're setting up the flag now." Just let things keep going that way, and no surprises, please. Neil and Buzz sound good, with no huffing and puffing to indicate they are overexerting themselves. But one surprise at least is in store. Houston comes on the air, not the slightest bit ruffled, and announces that the President of the United States would like to talk to Neil and Buzz. "That would be an honor," says Neil, with characteristic dignity.

The President's voice smoothly fills the air waves with the unaccustomed cadence of the speechmaker, trained to convey inspiration, or at least emotion, instead of our usual diet of numbers and reminders. "Neil and Buzz, I am talking to you by telephone from the Oval Office at the White House, and this certainly has to be the most historic telephone call ever made. . . . Because of what you have done, the heavens have become a part of man's world. As you talk to us from the Sea of Tranquility, it inspires us to redouble our efforts to bring peace and tranquility to Earth . . . " My God, I never thought of all this bringing peace and tranquility to anyone. As far as I am concerned, this voyage is fraught with hazards for the three of us—and especially two of us—and that is about as far as I have gotten in my thinking.

Neil, however, pauses long enough to give as well as he receives. "It's a great honor and privilege for us to be here, representing not only the United States but men of peace of all nations, and with interest and a curiosity and a vision for the future."

An American Teen "Moonstruck" in Germany

Deborah Sosin

In the following blog post, Deborah Sosin tells how fascinated she was by the plans for the moon landing when she was fifteen years old and had been collecting information about space and pictures of astronauts for years. She was particularly eager for the United States to beat the Soviets to the moon because she and her family lived in Germany and her father, whose organization beamed radio programs behind the Iron Curtain, was considered an enemy by the Soviets. It was the middle of the night in Germany when the landing was on television, and she was so excited after watching it that she couldn't sleep. This was partly because she was thinking about her new boyfriend, though—her emotions that summer were divided between her love life and the moon. Sosin is a writer, editor, and psychotherapist who maintains a blog at OpenSalon.com.

It was July 20th, 1969. My family crunched together on the couch watching our black-and-white German TV with the sound down. We leaned in close to catch every word on the Armed Forces Network radio broadcast.

Beep. "Roger. Go for landing, over. 3,000 feet." *Beep.*

My heart was pounding and my stomach was doing flip-flops. I could barely breathe. Part of me was going crazy waiting. And part of me was utterly distracted—reliving the sublime feeling of Heinrich Gerhardt's hands combing through my hair the night before.

Crackly voices spouted numbers and positions. "Four forward. 30 seconds. Contact light."

Then, "Houston, Tranquility Base here. The Eagle has landed."

I was fifteen years old and I was moonstruck. Although my obsession with boys was still blossoming, I'd been a NASA groupie for years. I knew all of the astronauts' names, and their wives' names. I collected 8 x 10 photos in a glossy two-pocket folder and pored over launch schedules and spacesuit diagrams. I memorized terms like "perihelion" and "translunar injection."

> My thoughts roared like waves, one over the other, remembering the moonwalk and Neil and Buzz and the flag and one giant leap for mankind.

My family had been living in Munich since 1966. My father was an executive with Radio Liberty, which beamed its programs behind the Iron Curtain. In those days, he was considered an enemy of the Soviets, so I was more eager than most Americans to beat the Russians.

By December 1968, the Apollo program was on course to land a man on the moon before the decade was out, as President [John F.] Kennedy had pledged. My romantic life, however, was on a bumpier trajectory. I wanted a boyfriend. When Franco Zeffirelli's movie *Romeo and Juliet* came out, I cried for the star-crossed lovers. I wrote sonnets about "souls that doth meet in heaven" and "my heart's anguish." And I cried on Christmas Eve, when Apollo 8 orbited the moon and [Frank] Borman, [James] Lovell, and [William] Anders shared their wistful message of hope and peace.

That winter, I resolved to launch my love life. I had a scorching crush on a German boy nicknamed Clipper, the shaggy-haired blond drummer in my brother's rock band. One day in March, Clipper slowly removed my floppy felt hat and Jackie O sunglasses, took my face in his hands, and kissed me. Shakespeare would've approved. In my diary, I wrote a three-page account of the scene, ending with the postscript, "Watched Apollo 9 splashdown! Can't *wait* for moon!"

The crescendo was building, in more ways than one.

In May, Apollo 10's lunar module, *Snoopy*, rehearsed maneuvers just ten miles above the moon's surface while the command ship, *Charlie Brown*, flew solo. I cheered but, sadly, my own maneuvers with Clipper had failed and I was unattached once more.

Counting the Days

Over the lazy June days after school was out, my best friend, Elaine, and I biked along the Isar River, chattering about boys and life and love, wondering about our future. Together, we counted the days until Apollo 11.

[Neil] Armstrong, [Buzz] Aldrin, and [Michael] Collins blasted off on July 16th. Three days later, around the time they entered the moon's gravitational field, Heinrich Gerhardt was driving me home in his green Citroën. Heinrich had long black hair and big teeth. He was no Romeo, but he was nineteen and funny and he liked me. We kissed, and kissed, goodnight. When he dropped me off, I hoped my parents didn't notice my rumpled hair and flushed cheeks.

The next night, the Eagle landed. It would take the astronauts a few hours to prepare for descent, so I went upstairs and napped. Dad woke me up to watch Armstrong climb down the ladder at 3:56 A.M. Man was on the moon!

The images were clear, but I don't remember what we said. I just knew the world had changed. It felt like everything was changing—new, irresistible forces of nature and gravity and history were beckoning me into their arms.

I tried to fall back asleep but couldn't. My thoughts roared like waves, one over the other, remembering the moonwalk and Neil and Buzz and the flag and one giant leap for mankind. And Heinrich.

Around noon, I called Elaine. "I've got moon fever!" I said.

"Me too!" she answered.

I hopped on my bike and pedaled to the neighborhood park. We rode around and around in circles, giddy as little girls, shouting, "Prepare for trans-sidewalk injection!" and "We have liftoff!"

When we got tired, we lay down on the soft grass, looked up at the sky, and talked about sex and Apollo and sex. We were fifteen. Nothing else mattered.

Listening to the Moon Landing on Radio in South Africa

Rob Nixon

At the time of the Apollo 11 moon landing, all television was banned in South Africa because the government feared that it would make people question the official system of apartheid, which required blacks to be segregated from whites. Like other South Africans, Rob Nixon and his family had to listen to the moon landing on the radio. He explains that so many people were upset by having to miss viewing the landing that later the government allowed tapes of it to be shown briefly. But whites went on campaigning against the TV ban, arguing that the lack of live coverage had made the nation look backward. The ban was eventually lifted, in part because advances in satellite technology had made it possible for anyone with a satellite dish to receive foreign transmissions. Nixon is a professor of English at the University of Wisconsin at Madison.

SOURCE. Rob Nixon, "Apollo 11, Apartheid, and TV," www .theatlantic.com, August 9, 2010. Copyright © 1999 by Rob Nixon. All rights reserved. Reproduced by permission.

On July 20 thirty years ago [as of 1999] my family—like millions of other South African families—was huddled around a crackling radio, listening to the moonwalk. Nobody in the entire country could watch it on TV. Television was verboten—a criminal technology under apartheid [racial segregation]. Not until 1976 did South Africa's first TV flicker into life.

I remember Neil Armstrong's epic stroll as the event that marked the beginning of the end for the apartheid government's conviction that South Africa could remain a fortress against television into the next millennium. By that time even the Americans, the government argued, would have recoiled from TV's innate degeneracy and returned to the more civilized pleasures of radio. Albert Hertzog, South Africa's Minister of Posts and Telegraphs from 1958 to 1968, warned the parliament that "inside the pill of TV there is the bitter poison which will ultimately mean the downfall of civilizations." Prime Minister Hendrik Verwoerd likened television to poison gas and the atom bomb. The little box was a threat "to the racial struggle on a global scale," he declared. "TV would cause absolute chaos to South African life."

But faced with the prospect of missing the moonwalk, even conservative white South Africans began to grumble. It was insulting, one senator declared, to be "bracketed with the most backward peoples of the world such as the Eskimos who have not got television." Travel operators capitalized on this discontent of the privileged, flying sold-out package tours to London: twelve hours there and twelve hours back for the illicit high of sitting in the Dorchester Hotel and watching the moon landing on TV.

> Some months after NASA's triumph, the government sought to quell local discontent by arranging limited viewings of the taped landing.

A Brief Look at Television

As a teenager I saw television just once, when, some months after NASA's triumph, the government sought to quell local discontent by arranging limited viewings of the taped landing. We had to line up at a planetarium: Mondays, Wednesdays, and Fridays for whites; Tuesdays and Thursdays for blacks. The turnout was immense. Policemen with German shepherds and Dobermans straining at the leash patrolled the line. After hours of waiting I entered a barricaded enclosure and joined twenty other people seated on collapsible metal chairs. A sullen moustached man tugged a sash, a purple velvet curtain slid back, and a television was revealed. For fifteen minutes I witnessed a lunar landing that seemed no stranger than the unearthly presence of that black box in the room. Then the curtain was closed again and we filed out, abandoning our seats to the next twenty people in line.

By the time I acquired my B.A., in African languages, I had spent no more than that solitary peepshow moment with a television. The year I graduated, apartheid's apparatchiks [officials blindly devoted to the system] cautiously introduced a single, state-controlled channel. . . .

After the Apollo landing whites campaigned in growing numbers to have the moratorium overturned. TV's absence, they protested, made South Africa look primitive. Black South Africans showed less interest in the debate: TV wasn't high on their list of deprivations. When the government finally capitulated, it did so in response not just to internal dissatisfaction but also to a new threat from abroad. NASA-led advances in satellite technology meant that foreign transmissions could now reach any South African with a concealed satellite dish and TV set. This possibility roused apocalyptic fears. One parliamentarian exclaimed, "Satellite broadcasts will be a mighty force in the hands of the Russians and Americans." Better to blanket the country with pro-apartheid TV as a preemptive strike. . . .

South African official Albert Hertzog (center) saw television as a "bitter poison" that must be kept out of his country. As a result, many in South Africa followed the moon mission only through radio reports. (**AP Images.**)

I have now lived in America for almost twenty years. I find that I seldom watch TV. I seem to lack the requisite forms of concentration—the media muscle memory— for a technology I acquired too late. Television fails to envelop me the way radio, books, and newspapers do; it's not something I can easily disappear into. But I look forward to the anniversary showings this month of Neil Armstrong's loopy underwater strides across the moon and across the tube. This time I'll be watching not in some poky booth patrolled by slavering dogs and armed guards but with a couch-sprawled nation for company. Still, I'm certain to feel some flickerings of my first sight of a TV set, and with it a frisson of illegality.

Memories of Meeting Neil Armstrong as a Teen

Bill Hilton, Jr.

In the following viewpoint, Bill Hilton tells how impressed he was with Neil Armstrong's presentation of the plans for the moon landing. He heard Armstrong speak at the National Youth Science Camp (NYSC), which Hilton attended as a high school student five years before the moon landing. By 1969 Hilton was back at NYSC as a director and watched the Apollo 11 launch with the staff. Lecturing at NYSC twenty years later, he expressed to the new generation of campers his wish that everyone could see Earth from a distance as the astronauts did and become aware of how small and fragile it is, and how important it is not to abuse it. Hilton is an educator-naturalist who was twice named South Carolina Science Teacher of the Year. He is now the director of the Hilton Pond Center for Piedmont Natural History, a nonprofit research and education organization.

SOURCE. Bill Hilton, Jr., "Memories of a Lunar Landing," www .hiltonpond.org, August 9, 2010. Copyright © 2003 by Hilton Pond Center. All rights reserved. Reproduced by permission.

Today [July 20, 1989] is a special day in the history of the U.S. space program, and people around the country are recollecting where they were 20 years ago when Neil Armstrong made his first small step onto the surface of the Moon in 1969.

I, too, have been thinking about that event, but my own memories of Armstrong go back five more years to 1964. That summer I was privileged to be among 100 high school scientists from around the country—two from each state—picked by their governors to attend the National Youth Science Camp [NYSC] at Bartow, West Virginia.

The NYSC was begun in 1963 to celebrate West Virginia's centennial, and in the years since plenty of top-notch, big-name scientists have visited the Mountain State to speak to NYSC delegates. None, however, could have had as much an impact on me as did the future astronaut who lectured in my camper year.

In July 1964 Neil Armstrong enthralled me and my fellow delegates with his presentation about futuristic plans for the Apollo manned mission to the Moon. I distinctly remember him standing before us outside the camp's rustic lecture hall, precise in his delivery and majestic in his professionalism and military bearing.

When I close my eyes I can still trace an image he drew on the chalkboard—a simple line drawing showing how the Apollo 11 module would need to fly a figure eight around Earth and Moon for a successful landing and eventual return trip. There Armstrong was—still five years away from his famous Moonwalk—already explaining and studying and practicing the moves he would execute to bring his lunar lander down at Tranquility Base. Talk about advance planning!

In the summer of 1969 I was back at the NYSC to direct the natural sciences program. By 16 July, that year's delegates had already returned home, so staff members gathered around the only available television set

> From a quarter million miles away [astronauts] have scanned our wispy clouds and our oceans and the continents of terra firma. . . . They understand, as can no others, how small a planet we inhabit.

at a small motel several miles from camp. We cheered and clapped at the successful liftoff of the giant Saturn rocket that propelled Apollo 11 out of Earth's atmosphere, and after that it was just a matter of waiting for Neil Armstrong and his colleagues to make their three-day trip to the Moon.

Shortly after the launch we closed camp for the season and I made a trip of my own back home to Rock Hill. A few evenings later I joined my parents and siblings in the TV room to watch Armstrong exit the lunar lander. Tears came to my eyes and a prideful lump filled my craw when I saw him make his first small footprint in dust that had never known a human's touch.

A Unique Perspective

Last week I returned to Bartow to celebrate my 25th anniversary as an NYSC delegate and to deliver my own lecture to this year's National Youth Science Camp. With cold chills crawling up and down my spine, I tried to convey to the current crop of campers how exciting it had been to meet Neil Armstrong 25 years earlier and to talk with him about his plans to be the first man on the Moon. I was nearly speechless at using the very same chalkboard my favorite astronaut had used in 1964.

Near the end of my lecture, I wished the science campers success in their upcoming college careers, and then I showed them a photograph of the Earthrise that Armstrong's crew had taken from the Moon. Neil Armstrong and all the other astronauts and cosmonauts have a unique perspective that none of the rest of us can really know. They have seen the "little blue marble" called Earth hanging in the immense black void of space. From a quarter million miles away they have scanned our wispy clouds and our oceans and the continents of terra firma that we walk upon each day. They understand, as can no others, how small a planet we inhabit, how delicate Spaceship Earth really is.

I closed my lecture with the wish that every 1989 science camper—and every Earthling, for that matter—could do as Neil Armstrong did and view our tiny planet from afar.

- Perhaps then we would all realize just how insignificant we are in this infinitely enormous universe.

- Perhaps then we would face the reality that this fragile planet, its environment, and its occupants can take only so much abuse.

- Perhaps then we could—with the same degree of confidence that Neil Armstrong showed in 1964—know what we will be doing five years into the future.

- And perhaps then that one small step by a man could finally become mankind's giant leap for peace and friendship among all nations on this lovely, little Planet Earth.

The Reaction to the Moon Landing in Russia

Sergei Khrushchev, interviewed by Saswato R. Das

In the following interview Sergei Khrushchev, the son of Nikita Khrushchev—who was the Soviet premier at the time of Apollo 11—discusses the Russian's reaction to the moon landing. They were not very interested in the landing, he says. In his opinion they felt much the same as Americans had when the Russian cosmonaut Yuri Gagarin became the first man to orbit Earth. Apollo 11 was mentioned in Soviet newspapers but was not shown on Russian television. He says that the Soviet Union was not close to getting to the moon (as NASA had believed they were) and could not have beaten the United States in the race to be first. His father did not understand why the leaders of the Soviet space program had failed. Sergei Khrushchev, who now resides in the United States, holds several advanced degrees in engineering and is a senior fellow in international relations at Brown University. Saswato R. Das is a science reporter based in New York.

SOURCE. Sergei Khrushchev, "The Moon Landing through Soviet Eyes," www.scientificamerican.com, October 20, 2010. Copyright © 2009 by Scientific American. All rights reserved. Reproduced by permission.

The Cold War between the U.S. and the U.S.S.R. formed the backdrop of the Apollo program, as the two superpowers jockeyed for preeminence in space. Under premier Nikita Khrushchev, the Soviet Union had succeeded in launching Sputnik 1, the first artificial satellite, and sending the first man [Yuri Gagarin] into orbit.

Reeling from a succession of Soviet space firsts, President John F. Kennedy promised that the U.S. would be first to send humans to the moon and return them to Earth before the end of the 1960s. On July 20, 1969, that promise came true as Americans claimed victory when Neil Armstrong and Buzz Aldrin walked on the moon, witnessed by some 500 million television viewers on Earth.

Sergei Khrushchev, Nikita's son, recently looked back and remembered what it felt like to be on the Soviet side. (These days, Khrushchev, 74, is a fellow at Brown University's Watson Institute for International Studies in Providence, R.I., where he spoke in his office, surrounded by Soviet memorabilia.)

An edited transcript of the interview follows.

Saswato R. Das: *Where were you when Neil Armstrong and Buzz Aldrin landed on the moon?*

Sergei Khrushchev: I remember the moon landing very well. I was 34. I was on vacation with my friends, most of whom worked at the Chelomei design bureau. There was also an officer from the KGB [Soviet secret police]. We were in Ukraine, in Chernobyl. It was exactly the place where they later built the [infamous] nuclear power station. The KGB officer had just returned from Africa, and he had brought a small telescope. So we looked through the telescope, but we didn't see any moon landing! So it was still questionable to us! [laughs]

How widely was the news of the moon landing disseminated in the Soviet Union in advance of the event?

Of course, you cannot have people land on the moon and just say nothing. It was published in all the newspapers. But if you remember [back then] when Americans spoke of the first man in space, they were always talking of "the first American in space" [not Yuri Gagarin]. The same feeling was prevalent in Russia. There were small articles when *Apollo 11* was launched. Actually, there was a small article on the first page of [Soviet newspaper] *Pravda* and then three columns on page five. I looked it up again.

> The Russian people had many problems in day-to-day life, they were not too concerned about the first man on the moon.

What was the mood in the Soviet space program when astronauts from Apollo 11 landed on the moon?

It was very similar to [the] feeling among Americans when Gagarin went into orbit. Some of them tried to ignore it, some of them were insulted. But I don't think it had a strong popular effect. First of all, the Soviet propaganda did not play it up or give too much information. I remember I watched a documentary on this. It was not secret, but it was not shown to the public. The Russian people had many problems in day-to-day life, they were not too concerned about the first man on the moon.

Was Russia pretty close?

The Russians were not pretty close. I think Russia had no chance to be ahead of the Americans under Sergei Korolev and his successor, Vasili Mishin. [Sergei Korolev was the leader of the Russian space program who, with Mishin overseeing the development of the rocket, succeeded in launching Sputnik 1. He died in January 1966.—Editor's Note]

Korolev was not a scientist, not a designer: he was a brilliant manager. Korolev's problem was his mentality. His intent was to somehow use the launcher he had. [The launcher was called N1. It was designed in 1958 for a different purpose and with a limited payload of about

Russian scholar Sergei Khrushchev says Soviet news minimized the US moon landing, just as Russia's space race wins were downplayed in the American press. (**M. Spencer Green/AP Images.**)

70 tons.] His philosophy was, let's not work by stages [as is usual in spacecraft design], but let's assemble everything and then try it. And at last it will work. There were several attempts and failures with *Lunnik* [a series of unmanned Soviet moon probes]. Sending man to the moon

is too complicated, too complex for such an approach. I think it was doomed from the very beginning.

Of course, you must understand that I am speaking from the point of a competitor. We worked with our own project, [at] the Chelomei design bureau. Maybe we were more realistic. But I don't think we would have been able to beat the Americans.

When talking about the Russian space program, there is a misconception in the West that it was centralized. In reality, it was more decentralized than in the United States, which had one focused Apollo program. In the Soviet Union, there were different designers who competed with one another.

What was your father's perspective on Apollo 11? Did you discuss with him the American moon landing over the years?

My father's reaction was he couldn't understand why Korolev failed in this race. And of course I gave him my opinion why. My father did not discuss [the moon landing] too much. He listened to me. He was very proud of Sputnik; he wrote about it in his memoirs.

What are your thoughts about renewed efforts to go to the moon?

The Apollo project was a political project. Now we are under very different circumstances. Also, a big difference is technological achievement. At that time, we were at the beginning of the age of [space] automation, discovery and research. Now we have all this, starting from the spectacular achievements of the Hubble Space Telescope and the Mars rovers, etc. I would give priority to automated vehicles, not manned spaceflight.

A Writer Reflects on the Moon Landing

Robert L. Forward

In the following viewpoint, written on the tenth anniversary of the Apollo 11 mission, the science fiction writer Robert L. Forward reflects on the excitement of the moon landing and how impressed he was by seeing that people all over the world were sharing it. That was a great time to be a human being, he says. But since then, the excitement has faded, although all the people he knows recall it with deep emotion. He is saddened by the retreat from further ventures into deep space and dismayed by the fact that humans are merely marking time—as they still are today, more than thirty years after he wrote this piece. Forward was a physicist and the author of many well-known science fiction novels.

SOURCE. Robert L. Forward, "On the Tenth of Apollo 11, Part 2," *Galileo*, September, 1979. Copyright © 1979 by Bob Forward. All rights reserved. Reproduced by permission.

It was great to be an American ten years ago [in 1969]. *We* had put a man on the Moon! Yet on that day—for the first time in my life—I felt that I was "more" than an American. I was part of the whole human race.

For someone who "never watched" television, the Apollo 11 landing on 20 July, 1969, became a 24-hour total experience in viewing. Sitting down with a pillow and plenty of provisions in front of my newly purchased television, I watched everything; every "simulated picture" animation and all the preambles, from the minute the networks came on the air to the closing commentaries of the pundits as the astronauts settled in for a night's rest.

The Excitement of Watching Humans in Space

The first excitement in the mission was the terrifying tension as the voices came crackling in from the rapidly dropping lander—the obvious fakeness of the network animations only heightening the apprehension.

"Two hundred feet, four-and-a-half down . . . kicking up some dust . . . four forward . . . drifting to the right a little . . . contact light . . . engine stop . . . " There was a long pause, then, "Houston, Tranquility Base here. The Eagle has landed!"

Finally came the time when the outer hatch door was dropped. The television camera attached to the door looked out on a smoothly rolly black and grey lunar horizon with the angular silhouette of the lander slashing its harsh black and white mechanical presence across one side of the screen.

In all the movies; in all the science fiction stories; in all the imaginings of what the first landing would be

> What really impressed me . . . were the live scenes bounced by communication satellites from countries in Europe and Asia, showing strange foreign faces as enraptured as I was by the miracle occurring on the television screens.

like; no one had ever imagined that it would be possible for the whole world to stand outside the newly arrived spaceship as the first man on the Moon laboriously worked his way out the hatch and down the ladder, and actually witness him taking the first step on the Moon!

What really impressed me as I waited for the astronauts to emerge, were the live scenes bounced by communication satellites from countries in Europe and Asia, showing strange foreign faces as enraptured as I was by the miracle occurring on the television screens in front of us. I looked at those faces, and finally it struck me. These weren't strange beings. They were humans—just like me. Each one of us, in order to be a participant in the wondrous event, had to drop our nationality, forget the color of our bodies, submerge our individualistic egocentric personalities, and become one with the lone human crawling backwards on hands and knees out of a too-narrow hatch—into the blazing vacuum of sunlit space.

An estimated ten thousand people gathered in New York's Central Park and watched the moon landing on giant TV screens. (**AP Images.**)

Then came their adventure out on the airless surface. Both men began bounding over the Moon's surface, busily setting up experiments. They didn't forget us, though. A ghostly apparition bounced toward the camera like a broken field runner, kicking up spurts of dust as he came. There was a moment of vertigo as the camera was taken from its fixture, then we, too, bounced across the surface until we were set up on our tripod so we could watch everything that went on.

> It will take many steps and much time before we again blast off into deep space. We need to get moving! But we wait—marking time.

It was a great time to be a human being. Nothing could stop us, nothing! More flights followed, each one more ambitious than before. But then something happened. The thrill that made it all worthwhile faded away and the miserly, pinched, cautious, scared little being that lurks within us all came to the fore.

Journeys into Deep Space Put on Hold

Like a little child playing out in the fields as night approaches, Apollo was called home. The journeys out into deep space were put on hold.

As the years have passed, my greatest discovery has been that the emotional involvement that I experienced in front of my television set was not mine alone. The same feeling came to everyone—the guard at the plant gate, my wife, the butcher, my 75-year-old mother—all get that same glowing gleam in their eyes whenever they relate their personal recollections of that event. Even today, you can see the same thrill of wonder in the eyes of young and old alike as they engage in the near-miraculous act of touching the Moon rock at the Air and Space Museum.

That moment—that rock—that Moon—belongs to all of us, and the lives of everyone on earth were touched and moved by those momentous years. [US president] John Kennedy knew how to reach that greatness that lies in every person, old or young, male or female, rich or poor. He reached past the squalor and greed, the natural cautiousness and fears, and drew that greatness out from the breast of this nation and used it to send us to the stars. We are all on this earth for only a short time. We all have to die sooner or later, why not do something interesting while we are here?

We have retreated back to Earth. The Space Shuttle is merely the first check item in the long countdown that will be needed to take us back out again, for the Shuttle will serve only to put us into a holding pattern in near-earth orbit. It is a long way back to the Moon, and an even longer distance to Mars. It will take many steps and much time before we again blast off into deep space. We need to get moving! But we wait—marking time.

T plus ten years . . . and still holding. . . .

GLOSSARY

Apollo 8   The first trip to the moon, during which astronauts orbited but did not land.

Apollo 11   The first moon landing mission. The name refers to the mission, not to the spacecraft.

Bay of Pigs   A 1961 incident involving a failed attempt by Cuban exiles to invade Cuba with support from the United States.

CapCom   Capsule Communicator, the astronaut on the ground assigned to handle all voice communications between astronauts in space and ground controllers.

Cape Kennedy   The area on the central Florida coast containing the Kennedy Space Center, from which American manned spacecraft are launched. This name was used between President John F. Kennedy's death in 1963 until 1973, when its original name of Cape Canaveral was restored.

Challenger   A space shuttle that disintegrated shortly after liftoff in January, 1986, resulting in the death of its crew. The accident was caused by flawed design of its solid rocket booster.

Columbia (1)   The command module for the Apollo 11 mission, which remained in orbit around the moon while the lunar lander went to surface.

Columbia (2)   A space shuttle that disintegrated during reentry in February, 2003, resulting in the death of its crew. The accident was caused by damage to its heat shield's tiles.

Command Module   The spacecraft occupied by the crew during an Apollo mission, which is docked with the lunar module while in flight.

Cosmonaut   A Russian astronaut.

CSM   Command/Service module, an Apollo command module combined with a service module that provides propulsion, electrical power and storage for consumables during a mission and is cast off before reentry into the atmosphere.

Cuban Missile Crisis   An event in October 1962 in which the Soviet Union placed missiles in Cuba, posing a danger to the United States. President John F. Kennedy persuaded the Soviets to remove them, but during this crisis, which lasted thirteen days, the two nations came close to war.

Eagle   The lunar lander module for the Apollo 11 mission.

EVA   An extra-vehicular activity, generally known to the public as a space walk.

Houston   The term usually used to refer to NASA's Johnson Space Center (JSC) in Houston, Texas (named for President Lyndon B. Johnson), which is used for design and development of spacecraft, training of astronauts, and ground control of spaceflights.

KSC   Kennedy Space Center, the NASA installation near Cape Canaveral, Florida, from which spacecraft are launched.

LEM or LM   The lunar lander, originally called a lunar excursion module and later simply a lunar module, that separates from an Apollo command module and descends to the surface of the moon.

Lunar Orbit Insertion   The orbital maneuver through which a spacecraft is placed in orbit around the moon.

NASA   The National Aeronautics and Space Administration, the US government agency responsible for the space program. It was established by act of Congress on July 29, 1958.

Reentry   The movement of a spacecraft from space back into the atmosphere, a process that requires protection from the extreme heat generated by atmospheric friction.

Saturn V
The expendable liquid-fueled booster rocket used for the Apollo launches. It was the largest and most powerful launch vehicle ever built, but further production was cancelled due to cost.

Sea of Tranquility
The area on the moon where the Eagle landed. Early astronomers thought the relatively dark markings on the moon (now known to be plains) were seas, and this area was given the name Mare Tranquillitatis. *Mare* is the Latin word for sea.

Space Race
The competition for supremacy in space achievements between the United States and the Soviet Union, lasting from the launch of Sputnik in 1957 until the Apollo 11 moon landing in 1969.

Space Shuttle
A US spacecraft in use since 1982 and scheduled to be retired in 2011. Technically, the term refers to the reusable orbiter (the crew module), its booster rockets, and its external fuel tank combined; but it is often applied to the orbiter alone. There are three remaining space shuttles, two of the original five having been destroyed in accidents. They are used for activities in Earth orbit and are not capable of reaching the moon.

Spin-off
As the term is used by NASA, a technological innovation that is the byproduct of a project rather than its intended goal.

Splashdown
The landing of a spacecraft by parachute in the ocean. All American spacecraft prior to the space shuttle returned in this way, and were recovered by helicopters onto navy ships.

Sputnik
The world's first artificial satellite, launched by the Soviet Union in October 1957 to the surprise and dismay of Americans, which led to the initiation of the Space Race.

Zero-g (zero-gravity)
Weightlessness experienced by astronauts in orbit. The term is not technically accurate because gravity exists in space; the weightlessness is produced by the fact that its pull is evenly balanced by the speed of the spacecraft as long as the spacecraft is not accelerating.

1957   October 4: The Soviet Union (USSR) launches Sputnik, the first artificial satellite.

November 3: The USSR launches Sputnik 2, carrying a small dog named Laika into orbit.

1958   January 31: Explorer 1 is launched and becomes the first US satellite.

1959   January 2: The USSR launches Luna 1, the first man-made object to escape Earth's gravity and the first lunar flyby.

March 3: Pioneer 4 is launched on a Earth-moon trajectory, passing within 37,000 miles of the moon.

September 12: The USSR launches Luna 2, the first man-made object to reach the surface of the moon.

October 4: The unmanned Soviet spacecraft Luna 3 orbits the moon and obtains the first photographs of its far side.

1960   April 1: Tiros 1, the first successful weather satellite, is launched.

1961   January 31: A chimpanzee named Ham becomes the first hominid in orbit. He performs simple tasks while aboard and is successfully recovered.

April 12: Soviet cosmonaut Yuri Gagarin orbits Earth,

becoming the first human in space.

May 5: On the first manned flight of the Mercury program, which is suborbital, Alan Shepard becomes the first American in space.

May 25: President John F. Kennedy addresses Congress and challenges the nation to go to the moon before the end of the decade.

1962   February 20: John Glenn becomes the first American to orbit Earth.

June 16: Cosmonaut Valentina Tereshkova becomes the first woman in space.

July 10: Telstar, the first commercially useful communications satellite, is launched.

August 11: The USSR launches Vostok 3 and 4, the first mission involving more than one spacecraft. Cosmonaut Andrian Nikolayev spends a record four days in space.

September 12: President Kennedy gives a speech at Rice University reaffirming the importance of the moon program.

1964   July 31: Ranger 7 transmits the first close-range images of the moon.

October 12: The USSR launches Voskhod 1 with a crew of three, the first spacecraft to carry more than one person.

1965   March 18: Cosmonaut Alexey Leonov becomes the first person to conduct a space walk.

March 23: Gus Grissom and John Young fly the first manned Gemini spacecraft.

June 3: Ed White becomes the first American to conduct a space walk.

December 4: Frank Borman and James Lovell begin a two-week stay in Earth orbit on Gemini 7.

December 15: Gemini 7 and Gemini 6, crewed by Walter Schirra and Thomas Stafford, make the first space rendezvous.

1966 February 3: The USSR's unmanned Luna 9 becomes the first spacecraft to soft-land on the moon.

March 16: Neil Armstrong and Dave Scott on Gemini 8 dock with an Agena rocket, achieving the first docking of two spacecraft in orbit.

April 3: The Soviet spacecraft Luna 10 enters lunar orbit, becoming the first satellite of the moon.

June 2: The unmanned spacecraft Surveyor 1 makes the first American soft landing on the moon.

August 14: Lunar Orbiter 1 enters orbit around the moon and takes the first picture of Earth from that distance (as a crescent, in black and white).

1967 January 27: In a ground test later designated Apollo 1, Gus Grissom, Ed White, and Roger Chaffee are killed when a fire ignites in their capsule.

April 24: Cosmonaut Vladimir Komarov is killed on Soyuz 1 when his parachute fails, making him the first person to die during a spaceflight.

November 9: Launch of Apollo 4, the first test of the Saturn V booster rocket.

1968   January 22: Launch of Apollo 5, an unmanned test of the Saturn and the lunar module.

April 4: Launch of Apollo 6, another unmanned test of the Saturn booster.

September 15: The USSR launches Zond 5, the first spacecraft to circle the moon and return to Earth. It carries turtles, which remain healthy.

October 11: Launch of Apollo 7, the first manned Apollo flight, which remains in orbit for ten days.

December 21: Launch of Apollo 8, the first manned journey to the moon.

December 24: Apollo 8 astronauts Frank Borman, James Lovell, and William Anders orbit the moon and transmit a Christmas Eve message to Earth on live television.

1969   January 16: The USSR's Soyuz 4 and 5 perform the first docking of two manned spacecraft and the first transfer of crews in space.

March 3: Apollo 9, the first manned flight of the lunar module, is launched into Earth orbit on a ten-day mission, also involving docking.

May 18: Apollo 10, a mission to test the lunar module while orbiting the moon, is launched, crewed by Thomas Stafford, John Young, and Eugene Cernan.

July 16: Apollo 11 is launched.

July 19: Apollo 11 goes into lunar orbit.

July 20: Neil Armstrong and Buzz Aldrin become the first men to walk on the moon, while Michael Collins orbits the moon alone in the command module.

July 21: The Soviet unmanned spacecraft Luna 15, which was intended to collect rock samples and return them to Earth, crash-lands on the moon several hours before Armstrong and Aldrin lift off.

July 24: Apollo 11 returns to Earth and is recovered after splashdown in the Pacific Ocean.

November 19: Apollo 12 astronauts Pete Gordon and Alan Bean walk on the moon.

1970   April 11–17: The Apollo 13 mission is aborted because of an explosion aboard the spacecraft in flight; James Lovell, Jack Swigert, and Fred Haise are forced to proceed to the moon and circle without landing, using the moon's gravity to acquire velocity for the return to Earth. Because the command module is low on power, they use the lunar module as a lifeboat, suffering great hardship due to shortage of consumables.

November 10: The USSR's Luna 17 lands an unmanned rover, Lunokhod, on the moon, where it remains functional for nine months.

1971   February 5: Apollo 14 astronauts Alan Shepard and Edgar Mitchell land on the moon.

June 30: Cosmonauts Georgi Dobrovolski, Viktor Patsayev, and Vladislav Volkov on Soyuz 11 make the first successful visit to a space station, Salyut 1, but die when their crew capsule accidentally depressurizes.

These are the only deaths to have occurred in space rather than in the high atmosphere.

July 30: Apollo 15 astronauts Dave Scott and James Irwin land on the moon, using the first lunar rover vehicle during their time on the surface.

1972   April 20: Apollo 16 astronauts John Young and Charles Duke make the first landing in the lunar highlands.

December 11: Apollo 17 astronauts Eugene Cernan and Harrison Schmitt make the last lunar landing.

1976   March: After many years of failure, the USSR abandons its attempts to develop the capability for sending a manned spacecraft to the moon.

1986   January 28: Seven Americans die when the space shuttle *Challenger* explodes and disintegrates shortly after liftoff.

1989   August 18: In an article in the Soviet government's official newspaper *Izvestiya*, the USSR acknowledges the former existence of its manned lunar program, which it had previously denied.

1998   January 7: Lunar Prospector, an unmanned probe, is launched.

March: Scientists announce that results from Lunar Prospector tests reveal the probable presence of water ice near the moon's poles.

2003   February 1: Another seven-member crew dies when the space shuttle *Columbia* disintegrates during reentry.

2009   June 18: The Lunar Reconnaissance Lander (LRO)

and LCROSS (Lunar Crater Observation and Sensing Satellite) are launched.

July 11–15: The LRO photographs the Apollo landing sites on the moon.

October 9: The LCROSS is deliberately crashed into the moon in order to send up a plume of dust and vapor that can be analyzed.

November 13: Scientists announce that the plume from the LCROSS crash contained water ice.

2010   October 21: Scientists announce that further analysis shows that there is significantly more water ice on the moon than was first thought, along with hydrogen and other useful elements.

FOR FURTHER READING

Books

Buzz Aldrin and Malcolm McConnell, *Men from Earth*. New York: Bantam, 1989.

Neil Armstrong, Michael Collins, and Edwin Aldrin, *First on the Moon*. Boston: Little, Brown, 1970.

Maria Benjamin, *Rocket Dreams: How the Space Age Shaped Our Vision of a World Beyond*. New York: Free Press, 2003.

Piers Bizony, *One Giant Leap: Apollo 11 Remembered*. Minneapolis: Zenith Press, 2009.

William E. Burroughs, *This New Ocean: The Story of the First Space Age*. New York: Random House, 1998.

Andrew Chaikin, *A Man on the Moon: The Voyages of the Apollo Astronauts*. New York: Viking Penguin, 1994.

Andrew Chaikin, *Voices from the Moon: Apollo Astronauts Describe Their Lunar Experiences*. New York: Viking Studio, 2009.

Michael Collins, *Carrying the Fire: An Astronaut's Journey*. New York: Farrar, Straus and Giroux, 2009.

Gerard J. DeGroot, *Dark Side of the Moon: The Magnificent Madness of the American Lunar Quest*. New York: New York University Press, 2006.

Francis French and Colin Burgess, *In the Shadow of the Moon: A Challenging Journey to Tranquility, 1965–1969*. Lincoln: University of Nebraska Press, 2007.

James R. Hansen, *First Man: The Life of Neil A. Armstrong*. New York: Simon & Schuster, 2005.

Robert Jacobs, *Apollo Through the Eyes of the Astronauts*. New York: Abrams, 2009.

Christopher Kraft, *Flight: My Life in Mission Control*. New York: Dutton, 2001.

Gene Kranz, *Failure Is Not an Option: Mission Control from Mercury to Apollo 13 and Beyond*. New York: Simon & Schuster, 2000.

Richard S. Lewis, *Appointment on the Moon*. New York: Ballantine, 1969.

Norman Mailer, *Of a Fire on the Moon*. Boston: Little, Brown, 1970.

Norman Mailer, *Moonfire: The Epic Journey of Apollo 11*. Los Angeles: Taschen, 2010.

Walter A. McDougall, *The Heavens and the Earth: A Political History of the Space Age*. New York: Basic Books, 1985.

Charles Murray and Catherine Bly Cox, *Apollo*. Burkittsville, MD: South Mountain Books, 2004. (Originally published as *Apollo: The Race to the Moon*. New York: Simon & Schuster, 1989.)

Craig Nelson, *Rocket Men: The Epic Story of the First Men on the Moon*. New York: Viking, 2009.

Robert Poole, *Earthrise: How Man First Saw the Earth*. New Haven: Yale University Press, 2010.

Alan Shepard and Deke Slayton, *Moon Shot: The Inside Story of America's Race to the Moon*. Atlanta: Turner Publishing, 1994.

Billy Watkins, *Apollo Moon Missions: The Unsung Heroes*. Lincoln: University of Nebraska Press, 2007.

Frank White, *The Overview Effect: Space Exploration and Human Evolution*. Boston: Houghton Mifflin, 1987.

Hugo Young, Bryan Silcock, and Peter Dunn, *Journey to Tranquility*. New York: Doubleday, 1970.

Periodicals

Neil A. Armstrong, "The Moon Had Been Awaiting Us a Long Time," *Life*, August 22, 1969.

Andre Balogh, "Above and Beyond: In 1969 Men Set Foot on the Moon for the First Time," *History Today*, July 2009.

William Borders, "Even in Hostile Nations, the Feat Inspires Awe," *New York Times*, July 22, 1969.

David Brittan, "The High Art of Apollo XI," *Technology Review*, July 1994.

Andrew Chaikin, "The Moon Voyagers," *Astronomy*, July 1994.

William J. Cook, Gareth G. Cook, and Jim A. Impoco, "When America Went to the Moon," *U.S. News & World Report*, July 3, 1994.

Henry S.F. Cooper, "Men on the Moon: Just One Big Rock Pile," *New Yorker*, April 12, 1969.

J.C. Crowther, "Beyond the Pillars of Hercules," *New Scientist*, July 17, 1969.

Gerard J. DeGroot, "The Dark Side of the Moon," *History Today*, March 2007.

John Dos Passos, "On the Way to the Moon Shot," *National Review*, February 9, 1971.

"Evolution into Space," *New York Times*, July 20, 1969.

Gene Farmer, "How Apollo 11 Changed Three Famous Men," *Life*, July 17, 1970.

Timothy Ferris, "Earthbound: Did the Moon Landing Turn Out to Be a Giant Leap to Nowhere?" *New Yorker*, August 1, 1994.

Tim Folger, Sarah Richardson, and Carl Zimmer, "Remembering Apollo," *Discover*, July 1994.

"Frontier Moon," *Economist*, July 19, 1969.

"A Ghost Town of Gantries," *Time*, April 15, 1974.

"The Great Adventure," *Newsweek*, July 21, 1969.

Sidney Hyman, "The Columbian Dilemma," *Bulletin of the Atomic Scientists*, September 1969.

Jeffrey Kluger, "Moon Walkers," *Time*, July 16, 2009.

Roger D. Launius, "Perceptions of Apollo: Myth, Nostalgia, Memory or All of the Above?" *Space Policy*, April 9, 2005. www.sciencedirect.com.

Lucas Laursen, "Tweeting the Lunar Landing," Forbes.com, July 16, 2009.

"The Legacy of Apollo 11," *Aviation Week & Space Technology*, July 17, 1989.

Richard S. Lewis, "End of Apollo: The Ambiguous Epic," *Bulletin of the Atomic Scientists*, December 1972.

John M. Logsdon and Alain Dupas, "Was the Race to the Moon Real?" *Scientific American*, June 1994.

Neil Mahr, "Neil Mahr on Shooting the Moon," *Environmental History*," Vol. 9 No. 3, 2004.

Richard Monastersky, "Shooting for the Moon: the Apollo Programme Inspired Thousands of People to Pursue Careers in Science," *Nature*, July 16, 2009.

"The Moon Landing Revisited," *American Enterprise*, July–August 1994.

"The Moon: Task Accomplished," *Time*, August 1, 1969.

Brian O'Leary, "In the Footprints of Apollo," *New Scientist*, July 19, 1979.

"Reactions to Man's Landing on the Moon Show Broad Variations in Opinions," *New York Times*, July 21, 1969.

James Reston, "New Dimension Added to History by Moon Landing," *New York Times*, July 21, 1969.

Jim Ridley, "Rocket Men," *Village Voice*, September 2007.

Harry Schwartz, "Space Program: Behind the Triumph, Criticism of Goals," *New York Times*, August 17, 1969.

Hugh Sidey, "Why We Went to the Moon," *Time*, July 25, 1994.

John Tierney, "Earthly Worries Supplant Euphoria of Moon Shots," *New York Times*, July 20, 1994.

"The Untold Story of Apollo 11," *Popular Mechanics*, June 2009.

Loudon Wainwright, "Apollo's Great Leap to the Moon," *Life*, July 25, 1969.

David Whitehouse, "Reach for the Moon," *New Statesman*, December 12, 1997.

John Noble Wilford, "Apollo as Mirage: 20 Years After the Moon Landing, A Sense of Mission Is Gone," *New York Times*, July 16, 1989.

John Noble Wilford, "On Hand for Space History, as Superpowers Spar," *New York Times*, July 13, 2009.

Tom Wolfe, "One Giant Leap to Nowhere," *New York Times*, July 18, 2009.

Websites

Apollo 11 at 40: Facts, Myths, Photos, and More (http://news.nationalgeographic.com/news/2009/07/090720-apollo-11-moon-facts.html). The *National Geographic*'s explanation of the facts that invalidate moon hoax myths, along with information about Apollo and photos.

Apollo: Humankind's First Steps on the Lunar Surface (www.nasa.gov/mission_pages/apollo). A NASA site developed for the fortieth anniversary of Apollo 11, which also covers the other moon landings. It includes interactive features, onboard audio from the missions, and photo galleries.

The Apollo Program (www.nasm.si.edu/collections/imagery/apollo/apollo.htm). Presentation by the National Air and Space Museum at the Smithsonian Institution, including pictures of objects in the museum's collection, podcasts of experts telling the stories behind them, videos, and more.

NASA History Program Office (http://history.nasa.gov/apollo.html). A site containing links to both NASA and non-NASA material about the Apollo program, including online editions of many full-length books.

National Space Society (www.nss.org). The website of the largest citizen's space advocacy organization contains an extensive library of online books and videos dealing with planned and proposed space projects. It has an emphasis on the use of the moon and other extraterrestrial resources to benefit the Earth as well as on future space settlement. It also offers book reviews, articles from its magazine *Ad Astra*, and links to other space sites.

One Giant Leap for Mankind (history.nasa.gov/ap11-35ann). A NASA website created on the thirty-fifth anniversary of the Apollo 11 mission to honor all those involved in its success. It contains astronaut comments, biographies, bibliographies, image and video galleries, and many other resources, including the text of all seventy-three goodwill messages from foreign leaders for the silicon disc that was left on the moon.

Space Race (www.nasm.si.edu/exhibitions/gal114/gal114.htm). An exhibition at the National Air and Space Museum with information about both US and Soviet achievements in space during the Cold War.

Students for the Exploration and Development of Space (www.seds.org). An independent, student-based organization that promotes the exploration and development of space by educating people about the benefits of space and supporting a network of interested students. It encourages high school as well as college chapters.

To the Moon (www.pbs.org/wgbh/nova/tothemoon). Companion site to the two-hour PBS *Nova* special "To the Moon," which was broadcast in July 1999 and is also available on DVD.

We Choose the Moon (wechoosethemoon.org). An interactive multimedia re-creation of the Apollo 11 mission, including video, recordings, archival photos, and other items. Produced by AOL.

Where Were You? (www.wherewereyou.com). Personal memories with various points of view from people who were alive during the Apollo 11 moon landing. The site encourages submissions from individuals and from younger people who have interviewed friends or relatives.

INDEX

West Germany, 36

West Virginia, 169

Westinghouse, 57

White, Ed, 16

Whole Earth Catalog, 119

Wilson, Harold, 35

Women in space, 5

Worden, Alfred, 128t

World War I, 5

World War II, 5–6, 14, 18, 95

Worster, Donald, 117

Y

Yankee Clipper (lunar command module), 128t

Young, Hugo, 83–92

Young, John, 8, 128t

Yugoslavia, 32

Z

Zambia, 26

Zeffirelli, Franco, 160